Google Certified Educator Level 1
Strategies, Practice & Review
2018-2019

By: Brannon Fissette

ISBN: 9781718014640

DEDICATION

To the teachers that I have worked with day in and day out in my short career in education. Your work is truly inspiring, and I could not do it, it is way too exhausting.

For Tricia, Edward and, Elisabeth I could not have asked for a more supporting and loving family.

The Google Certified Educator Level 1 course contains two sections, a multiple-choice section and a practical. Test takers have three hours to complete both sections.

This book contains strategies and tricks on passing both the Question/Answer & Scenario section of the test.

Section 1: Google Terms & Apps
Common Google Terminology as well as a brief description of the various google applications.

Section 2: Question and Answer Strategies
In this section we will explore several questions that are like those found on the certification exam and go step by step in how to find the correct answer.

Section 3: Practical
The meat and potatoes of the exam is the Practical. We will look at several scenarios that are like those found on the exam and walk through how to solve them

Section 4: Practice Questions
Test your Google knowledge on these practice questions that are in the same style as the exam questions

Section 5: Questions Answer Key
Check your work – also some insight on why some answers are correct or incorrect.

Section 6: Practice Scenarios
Five Scenarios with multiple tasks each will test your practical working knowledge of the Google Suite.

Section 7: Practical Answer Key
Check to see if you got the same result on the Scenarios. If you did not, go back and try again!

Section 9: Final tips and tricks
These are some of the tips and tricks that have helped me pass the exam and train others on passing as well.

Good Luck!

Table of Contents

Section 1 – Google Terms and Apps

Terminology

Application Array: The nine-dot button at the top right of Google Applications – this button allows you to go to google applications

Chrome Omnibox: The place where you type a web address or search within Chrome

Digital Citizenship: The practice of safe, responsible and legal use of technology

Google Certified Apps Administrator

Google Certified Educator

Google Certified Innovator

Google Certified Trainer

Personal Learning Network: An informal network of individuals that a person uses to gain knowledge

Sharing: Giving permission for another user to view, edit, or comment on a document (also can be termed as "to share" or "to collaborate"

Add-on: Features developed by third-parties to enhance the functionality of Google Applications (Docs, Sheets, Slides etc.)

Apps: Applications developed b third-party developers that run using the Chrome browser or on a Chromebook (examples: Speedtest, Zoom, Scratch Jr.)

Extensions: Features developed by third-parties to enhance the functionality of Google Chrome (examples: Save to Drive, Save to Classroom)

Google Applications

Just like with any other computer program or website there are multiple ways to get around the Google Suite. You can sign in via the Chrome web browser or through one of the Google Suite apps. I recommend signing in through Google Drive.

https://Drive.Google.com

Once you sign into Google Drive you will be placed right in your file   repository

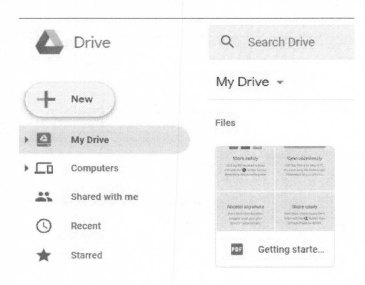

From here you will be able to create files, upload files, as well acccess all of the other Google Sutie applications.

Depending on your domain and permissions you will have access to the below applications:

Application	Description

	My Account Change your password Update your information Setup Account Preferences
	Blogger Create Blogs Explore Blogger Communities
	Google Calendar Schedule your day Create appointment slots View holidays
	Chromecast Mirror Chromebook displays on your monitor
	Chrome Store Install extensions and applications from the Chrome web store
	Google Contacts Manage your email contacts Create contact lists Store information about contacts
	Google Docs Word processor Collaborate in real time
	Google Drive File repository Where Google application documents are saved
	Google Earth View the earth from Satellite to Street level views. Zoom in just about anywhere
	Google Finance Check the Stock Market Read financial news
	Google Forms Create surveys, quizzes and sign-up sheets
	Gmail Email platform Communicate
	Google Classroom Online learning platform Post Assignments

	Built in Gradebook
	Google Cloud Print Print to network printers form Chromebooks or the Chrome Application
	Google Expeditions Virtual Reality field trips View the world through a new lens
	Google Groups Create discussion boards Send Group Emails
	Google Play Store Install Android applications within Chrome View movies and listen to music
	Google+ Google's Social Networking Platform Join communities Share what's important
	Google Hangouts Create video chats Talk within documents
	Google Keep Billboard for your thoughts Share with your network
	Google Maps 2D Maps and Directions Free Navigation with your phone
	News Aggregated news from around the internet
	Google Photos Organize, save and view your photos
	Google Scholar Search, view, and explore scholarly articles from journals and publications. Easily create citations and manage your sources
	Google Sheets Collaborative Spreadsheets Create charts and graphs and analyze data
	Google Sites Create dynamic web sites with drag and drop editing

	Google Slides Google's presentation software Create and animate slide shows Embed Videos and more
	Google Translate Translate texts between languages Even translate entire websites!
	Google Voice Create a unique phone number managed by Google Listen to and transcribe voicemails
	YouTube Search and view videos from almost every topic Share your creations

To access any of these tools from within Google Drive (or any other Google application) click the app array

If you do not see the app listed select "Even more from Google".

If you still do not see the application listed, your Domain Administrator may have it turned off.

Section 2 - Question / Answer section

The question/answer section contains multiple choice questions along with drag and drop matching or organizing question types.

Pay attention to the LANGUAGE being used in the question. The questions will lead you to the correct answer, if you read carefully and have a basic understanding of the material. This section has been described as more of a language comprehension exam more than a knowledge test.

Let's examine a couple different questions and determine the answer based on the language being used.

Sample Question 1
Multiple Choice Question
Please select 4
You are teaching a course on chemistry, what digital activities can you use to help enhance your lesson?
- ☐ Use Google Sites to create a website about the chemical processes being examined
- ☐ Watch YouTube videos about the chemical composition of a beverage
- ☐ Create a drawing of the chemical structure using Google Drawings
- ☐ Find an example of a chemical process in your textbook and read them to your students
- ☐ Use the Explore tool in Google Slides to add a picture of the chemical to a presentation

Now examine the question and pick out the key word(s) for the answer.

> You are teaching a course on chemistry, what **digital activities** can you use to help enhance your lesson?

Even if you are unaware of how to use the Google suite of tools, by examining the answers you can deduce that there is only one activity listed that is not digital.

- ☑ Find an example of a chemical process in your textbook and read them to your students

The certification test will always give you the amount of correct answers:
Multiple Choice Question
Please select 4

Now, you know that there are four correct answers out of five. You were also able to determine the one answer that does not meet the question criteria based of the key words. Congratulations, you got the first question correct!

Sample Question 1 - Answer
Multiple Choice Question
Please select 4
You are teaching a course on chemistry, what digital activities can you use to help enhance your lesson?
- ☑ Use Google Sites to create a website about the chemical processes being examined

☑ Watch **YouTube** videos about the chemical composition of a beverage
☑ Create a drawing of the chemical structure using Google Drawings
☐ Find an example of a chemical process in your textbook and read them to your students
☑ Use the Explore tool in Google Slides to add a picture of the chemical to a presentation

Now let's try another:

Sample Question 2

Multiple Choice Question
Please select 3
You have lost a very important email from one of your students' parents! How can you use the search function in Gmail to locate that email?
☐ Search for the emails sender
☐ Search for a keyword in the email, such as the student's name
☐ Search for the word count of the email
☐ Search for emails that were sent to you
☐ Search for a label applied to the email (example: parents)

This question is a little bit trickier. First let's see if we can narrow down the correct answers by eliminating one of the nonsense answers.

☐ Search for the word count of the email

Gmail does not allow you to search via word count. But, even if you did not know that, think about how insane that would be. If you knew the email contained 456 words - then not only is your memory outstanding and you could probably dictate the email by heart, but there may be a ton of emails with a similar word count.

Now out of the remaining answers, three are the "Correct" answer, but all of them are technically correct. How can we narrow it down further?
☐ Search for the emails sender
☐ Search for a keyword in the email, such as the student's name
☐ ~~Search for the word count of the email~~
☐ Search for emails that were sent to you
☐ Search for a label applied to the email (example: parents)

Think about each response independently for a second.
☐ Search for the emails sender
If you searched for the person's name who sent you the email it would only bring back the emails from that individual - if they do not send you hundreds of emails a week this will narrow down the results.

Google   from: brannon| 🔍

Gmail ▾   ☐ ▾   ↻   More ▾

☐ Search for a keyword in the email, such as the student's name

By searching for the student in question you can trim the amount of results to a manageable few (or few dozen).

☐ Search for emails that were sent to you

By searching all emails that were sent to you, would show you EVERYTHING already in your inbox or labeled folders... So, while possible, it will not shorten your search any. So, we can mark this answer as one of the possible incorrect answers.

☐ Search for a label applied to the email (example: parents)

If you labeled the email, or created a rule to automatically label emails from parents by searching through those you will for sure have a shorter list of emails to go through.

By examining each answer for a few seconds, we can now more easily choose the correct answer for the question:

Sample Question 2 - Answer
Multiple Choice Question
Please select 3
You have lost a very important email from one of your students' parents! How can you use the search function in Gmail to locate that email?
    ☑ Search for the emails sender
    ☑ Search for a keyword in the email, such as the student's name
    ☐ Search for the word count of the email **- Would bring up too many results**
    ☐ Search for emails that were sent to you **- Not possible in Gmail**
    ☑ Search for a label applied to the email (example: parents)

Now, let's examine a couple of matching (drag & drop) questions that are in this section as well.

Sample Question 3
Drag & Drop Question
Google has a variety of tools that give educators a ton of flexibility in the classroom. Match the Google Tool with its function

Function	**Tool**
1. Create and manage assignments, with a "turn in" button	a. Slides
2. Create Presentations, or slide decks	b. Sheets
3. Manipulate data and use mathematical functions	c. Docs
4. Create a website for your class	d. Sites
5. A collaborative word processor	e. Classroom

The first step in this type of question is to line up what you already know. Based on your experience you know that Google docs is a word processor, and that Slides allows you to make presentations
.

Function	**Tool**
1. Create and manage assignments, with a "turn in" button	a. Slides
2. Create Presentations, or slide decks	b. Sheets
3. Manipulate data and use mathematical functions	c. Docs
4. Create a website for your class	d. Sites
5. A collaborative word processor	e. Classroom

Now, let's look at the language being used and search for Keywords, or words that stand out.

Create a **website** for your class

The keyword in this short statement is **website** - what tool sounds like it can create a website? Google Sites!

Manipulate **data** and use mathematical **functions**

When you work with **data** - lists of numbers / dates / names etc. There is one tool that will allow you to sort, chart, arrange, and use mathematical functions; Google Sheets. Google sheets is the spreadsheet application bundled together in the Google Suite.

Tip: When you run across any question with Google Sheets as an answer - think *DATA* and *ANALYSIS*.

Function   Tool

1. Create and manage assignments, with a "turn in" button   a. Slides
2. Create Presentations, or slide decks   b. Sheets
3. Manipulate data and use mathematical functions   c. Docs
4. Create a website for your class   d. Sites
5. A collaborative word processor   e. Classroom

Now we have only one answer left to match:

Create and manage assignments, with a "turn in" button

Using the last Tool available we can match that up. The certification test will never give you more options to choose from, or let you duplicate answers on this type of question.

Sample Question 3 - Answer
Drag & Drop Question
Google has a variety of tools that give educators a ton of flexibility in the classroom. Match the Google Tool with its function

Function   Tool

1. Create and manage assignments, with a "turn in" button   a. Slides
2. Create Presentations, or slide decks   b. Sheets
3. Manipulate data and use mathematical functions   c. Docs
4. Create a website for your class   d. Sites
5. A collaborative word processor   e. Classroom

The next type of Drag & Drop question tasks you with categorizing items either based on their name or the process. Let's look at a couple of those.

Sample Question 4
Drag & Drop Question
When working with a student on their capstone project, you have suggested that they use a couple of different applications to make their project more dynamic. Use Drag and drop to show how the student can use the Google Applications to make their capstone project memorable.

Google Application	How to Use
Google Forms	Create a survey to share with peers
	Diagram the processes within the project
	Give a quiz to participants
Google Drawings	Display content in a dynamic way for viewers
	Host all capstone materials in an easy to navigate page
Google Sites	

In this question, there are three applications to choose from; **Google Forms**, **Google Drawings** and, **Google Sites.** There are however, only five "how to use" items to choose from. This means that the "how to use" items will not easily distribute between the applications.

Just like in the previous Drag & Drop example, let's start off with what we know.

Create a **survey** to share with peers

Using our experience has taught us that Google Forms, allows you a quick and easy way to create a survey.

Google Application	How to Use
Google Forms	
Create a survey to share with peers	Diagram the processes within the project
	Give a quiz to participants
Google Drawings	Display content in a dynamic way for viewers
	Host all capstone materials in an easy to navigate page
Google Sites	

Now let's look for some keywords.

Host all capstone materials in an easy to **navigate page**

When I see, the words navigate and, page I think of websites – and browsing webpages. **Google Sites** allows you to create easy websites and by extension webpages.

Give a **quiz** to participants

A **quiz** is a just survey with right or wrong answers. You could host a quiz on a website, but you first will need to create it using a **Google Form**.

Google Application	How to Use
Google Forms	
Create a survey to share with peers	Diagram the processes within the project
Give a quiz to participants	
Google Drawings	Display content in a dynamic way for viewers
Google Sites	
Host all capstone materials in an easy to navigate page	

Now we have only two answers remaining.

Display content in a dynamic way for viewers

There are several ways to get content to users; create a slide show, email them, create a video and share it on **YouTube** etc. Another way to share content is through a website, **Google Sites** will allow you to create a website to share with viewers.

Diagram the processes within the project

This one is a bit tricky. When diagraming a process some word processors allow you to create flow charts to display the information in a visually appealing manner. Google Docs does not have the flow chart functionality built into it. Instead they have an application called **Google Drawings**, which allows you to create flow charts and diagrams with different shapes by drawing them onto a canvas.

To launch Google Drawings within a Google Document, select the **Insert** tab and then choose **Drawing...**
Or you can go to **https://drawings.google.com** for the stand-alone application.

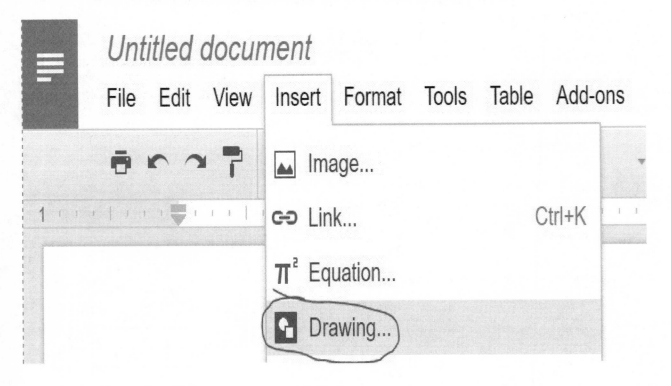

Sample Question 4 - Answer
Drag & Drop Question
When working with a student on their capstone project, you have suggested that they use a couple of different applications to make their project more dynamic. Use Drag and drop to show how the student can use the Google Applications to make their capstone project memorable.

Google Application	How to Use
Google Forms	
Create a survey to share with peers	
Give a quiz to participants	
Google Drawings	
Diagram the processes within the project	
Google Sites	
Host all capstone materials in an easy to navigate page	
Display content in a dynamic way for viewers	

Now let's do one more Drag & Drop style of question with more abstract concepts.

Sample Question 5

Drag & Drop Question
Your administration is really starting to get onboard with utilizing the Google Suite at your campus, however they need to convince the board of directors to adapt. You have been tasked with comparing the characteristics of Digital Media vs. Physical Textbooks. Place the correct benefit underneath its rightful category to highlight its characteristics.

Category	Characteristic
Digital Technology	Information can be updated constantly
	Can take up valuable physical space
	Limited amount of accessibility options
	Information is available in multiple formats
	Information can easily go out of date
Physical Textbooks	Research materials may need to stay on campus to protect school property
	A wide variety of information available to challenge or support subjects

This is an example of a question that exam will ask to highlight the benefits of using the Google Suite of applications without naming them. When you see a question of this type as a tip look at the positive responses first and categorize those as digital and any negative responses as physical. For example:

Limited amount of accessibility options

Just like in the other questions, looking at the keyword Limited, we can tell this is a negative response. Anything that limits students is not good. If you put yourself in the shoes of a Google test creator, would you want to paint your product in a negative light? Additionally, accessibility options are a benefit to digital content. For example, being able to change the size of text, having the computer read to you and, adjusting the contrast can all be done on a digital device but not in a textbook. This characteristic is for a **Physical Textbook**.

Now let's look at a positive characteristic.

Information can be updated constantly

The fact that you will not need to purchase a new textbook if something needs to be updated is a huge win for **Digital Content**. Websites and applications are constantly being updated with the latest information and provide a valuable resource for students.

Category	Characteristic
Digital Content	
Information can be updated constantly	Can take up valuable physical space
	Information is available in multiple formats
	Information can easily go out of date
Physical Textbooks	Research materials may need to stay on campus to protect school property
Limited amount of accessibility options	A wide variety of information available to challenge or support subjects

Now let's look at the other characteristics that are leftover and see if we can categorize them as positive (digital) vs. negative (physical).

Can take up valuable **physical** space

A huge negative if space is an issue. Classroom bookshelves can become overcrowded with out of date textbooks and materials over time. Digital content does not take up physical space so this is a characteristic of a **Physical textbook**. Additionally, notice the keyword Physical inside the answer.

Information can easily go out of date

Out of date information is a red flag, automatically negative. This is also the flipside to "Information can be updated constantly", which we determined to be a digital characteristic. So, we can file this characteristic under **Physical Textbook**.

A wide variety of information available to challenge or support subjects

This a big positive for **Digital Content**. Having multiple sources available to students allows them to explore different viewpoints and support their arguments that much better. Having a limited number of textbooks on a subject can hinder a student's understanding of a topic.

Category	Characteristic
Digital Content	
Information can be updated constantly	
A wide variety of information available to challenge or support subjects	
	Information is available in multiple formats
Physical Textbooks	Research materials may need to stay on campus to protect school property
Limited amount of accessibility options	
Can take up valuable physical space	
Information can easily go out of date	

Alright, we are almost there. Let's look at the last two characteristics available and see if we can place them in the correct category.

Research materials may need to stay on campus to protect school property

If a school is worried about items leaving campus, then that is a physical item. While electronic devices are physical – the digital content on them is not. This category would be filed under **Physical Textbook**, as digital content does not take up any physical space and it would not matter if it is removed from campus.

Information is available in multiple formats

While textbooks may be available in several formats or languages, this is a positive answer and one that the Test creators will want you to place under the **Digital Content**. Digital content can be videos, audio, text, even virtual reality. The sheer number of formats available is a benefit to **Digital Content** and one that Google wants to highlight.

Sample Question 5 - Answer

Drag & Drop Question

Your administration is really starting to get onboard with utilizing the Google Suite at your campus, however they need to convince the board of directors to adapt. You have been tasked with comparing the characteristics of Digital Media vs. Physical Textbooks. Place the correct benefit underneath its rightful category to highlight its characteristics.

Category	Characteristic
Digital Content	
Information can be updated constantly	
A wide variety of information available to challenge or support subjects	
Information is available in multiple formats	
Physical Textbooks	
Limited amount of accessibility options	
Can take up valuable physical space	
Information can easily go out of date	
Research materials may need to stay on campus to protect school property	

Section 3 – Practical

The second part of the certification exam is where the real fun begins, the practical. You will login to the test with a Google account generated by Google. You will then be given several multi-part scenarios that will have you use the Google account within the Google Suite. These scenarios are meant to test and challenge your understanding of how to use the different Google Applications. Let's look at a couple of examples.

Sample Scenario 1 – Task 1

Task 1 of 2

Your mailbox has become inundated with emails from administration, parents and mailing lists. You are overwhelmed, but you know there is a better way. You decide to spend some time and organize your mailbox with labels.

Go to your inbox and label the following emails with **Parent**, **Administration**, or **Mailing Lists**.

From Principal Brannon, requesting paperwork (Administration)
From Mrs. Fissette, issue with teaching style (Parent)
From Mr. Smith, question about Google Suite (Mailing Lists)

To complete this Scenario, you will need to go into the testing accounts Gmail. You can do this a couple of different ways:

Navigate to

https://gmail.com

https://mail.google.com

or

if you are already on another Google Application select the Apps Icon and choose Gmail.

When you get to Gmail, you will see the emails listed in the question:

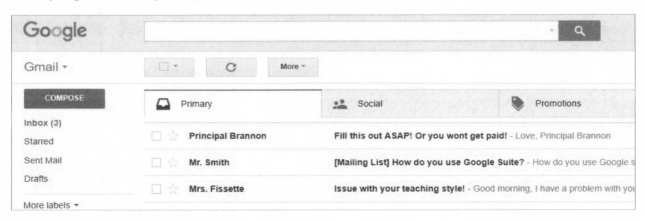

Check the first email from **Principal Brannon,** it will become highlighted.

Choose the Label Icon and then Select "Create New"

Type in **Administration** (tip: if you are a bad speller use Copy & Paste to ensure you get it exactly right) and select Create

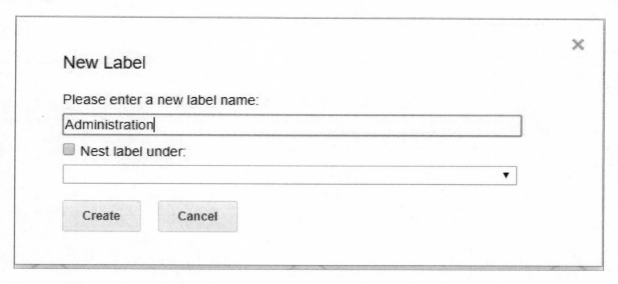

If done properly, you will see the label applied to the email:

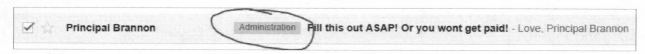

Now, uncheck the email from Principal Brannon and do the same thing for the other two emails with the proper Labels; **Parent** or **Mailing Lists.** When completed your inbox should look like this:

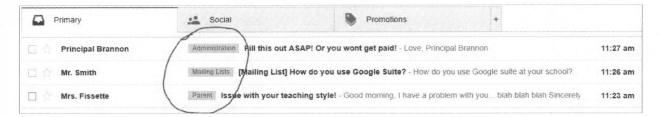

This Scenario has two tasks to it, let's look at the next task.

Sample Scenario 1 – Task 2

Task 2 of 2

It seems like the email from Principal Brannon is very important and you should probably set a reminder to remember to take care of it.

Go to your inbox and find the email from Principal Brannon – Create a Task from this email.
Set a Due Date for some time before the end of the week.
Add a note that says "Very Important!"

To complete this task, you will need to be in the testing accounts inbox. Start off by selecting the email from Principal Brannon.

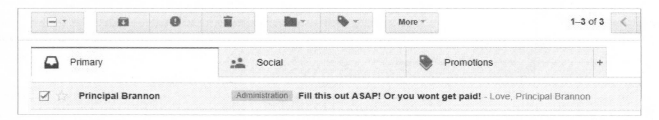

Now select the **More** drop-down box and choose **Add to Tasks**

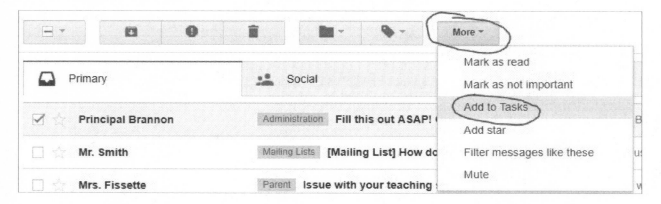

At the bottom, left corner of yours screen the task window will Pop-in

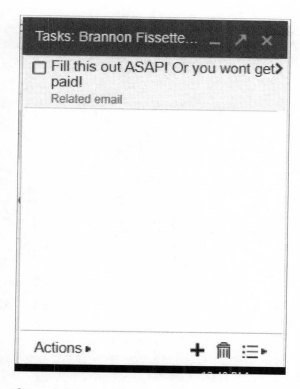

If you do not see the Task Window, Select Tasks from the Gmail Drop down button (Top Left of the screen)

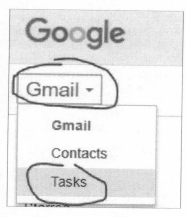

Now that you have the task created, you need to add a Due Date and a note. To do this select the > icon next to the task.

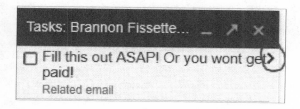

Select the Due Date with the **Calendar** Icon next to the **Due Date** field. Then enter a note into the **Notes** Section. When completed select the **Back to List** link to save the Task

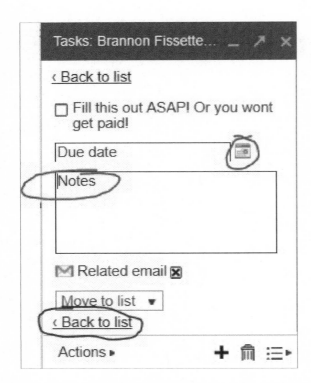

Your Task should look something like this when completed:

Congratulations, you have completed the first Scenario. You will NOT know if you did the task completely or correctly until you submit your exam at the end. When you are confident that you completed the tasks correctly move on to the next scenario.

This next sample Scenario will be using a different Google application, let's look!

Sample Scenario 2 – Task 1

Task 1 of 3

Report cards are due in a few days and you have been Biology Classes grades in a Google Sheet. Analyze the data to see where your currents currently stand in Biology.

Open the **Biology Grades** sheet and calculate the students Final Grade by averaging their test scores.

This Scenario has three tasks to complete. The initial task asks that you open the **Biology Grades** sheet and to average the student's grades. The Biology Grades sheet will be located with the **Exam Materials** folder in the testing accounts Google Drive. You can access Google Drive by the following different ways:

Navigate to

https://drive.google.com

or

Select the "Open Exam Materials" button located below the Scenario Description (in the live test)

or

if you are already on another Google Application select the Apps Icon and choose Drive.

Open the **Exam Materials** Folder and then locate the **Biology Grades** sheet and open it.

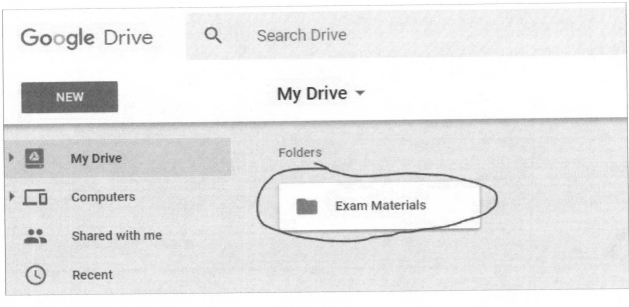

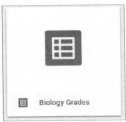

Once you have the sheet open, you will be presented with the data from several student's grades. There will be a column available to enter the average grade.

Biology Grades ☆ 📁

File   Edit   View   Insert   Format   Data   Tools   Add-ons   Help   All changes saved in Drive

	Student	Grade 1	Grade 2	Grade 3	Grade 4	Average
2	Susan	77	60	55	97	
3	SMith	55	66	77	88	
4	Sam	0	76	0	89	
5	bill	99	98	100	97	
6	John	88	98	76	94	
7	Sam	88	98	67	87	
8	Edward	100	99	100	90	
9	Elisabeth	100	100	99	100	

Select the Row 2, Column F cell to enter the first average (F2)

	A	B	C	D	E	F
1	Student	Grade 1	Grade 2	Grade 3	Grade 4	Average
2	Susan	77	60	55	97	

In cell F2 enter the following:

=Average(b2:e2)

fx =Average(B2:E2)

	A	B	C	D	E	F
1	Student	Grade 1	Grade 2	Grade 3	Grade 4	Average
2	Susan	77	60	55	97	72.25

Or

=Average(b2,c2,d2,e2)

=Average(B2,C2,D2,E2)

A	B	C	D	E	F
Student	Grade 1	Grade 2	Grade 3	Grade 4	Average
Susan	77	60	55	97	72.25

To average the rest of the students quickly – double click on the dot at the bottom right corner of the cell

fx =Average(B2:E2)

	A	B	C	D	E	F
1	Student	Grade 1	Grade 2	Grade 3	Grade 4	Average
2	Susan	77	60	55	97	72.25

	A	B	C	D	E	F
1	Student	Grade 1	Grade 2	Grade 3	Grade 4	Average
2	Susan	77	60	55	97	72.25
3	SMith	55	66	77	88	71.5
4	Sam	0	76	0	89	41.25
5	bill	99	98	100	97	98.5
6	John	88	98	76	94	89
7	Sam	88	98	67	87	85
8	Edward	100	99	100	90	97.25
9	Elisabeth	100	100	99	100	99.66666667

Or you can either enter the formula again manually (time consuming).

Task one completed, now onto Task 2.

Sample Scenario 2 – Task 2

Task 2 of 3

Principal Brannon is very interested in your Biology class report card, he would like to see the data that you have collected so far, along with a chart that shows the data in a visually appealing way.

Share the **Biology Grades** sheet with Principal Brannon

Create a chart of the students grades on the **Biology Grades** sheet

---

With the **Biology Grades** sheet, still open, select the **Share** Button (top right corner)

In the People field type Princial Brannon followed by the Enter Key

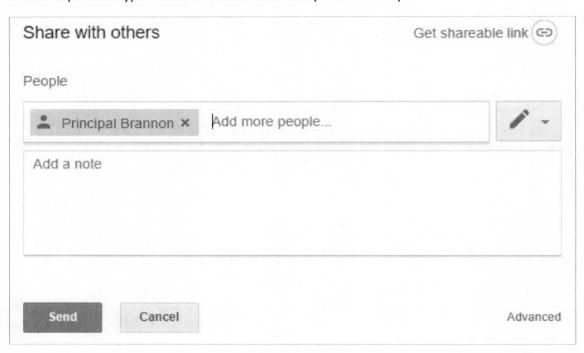

Tip: If it does not specifically say what type of rights to give (view only, edit, comment) stick with the default.

Click the **Send** Button

To check to see if the Share was successful, click the **Share** button once again. You will see Principal Brannon listed under the **Shared With** section

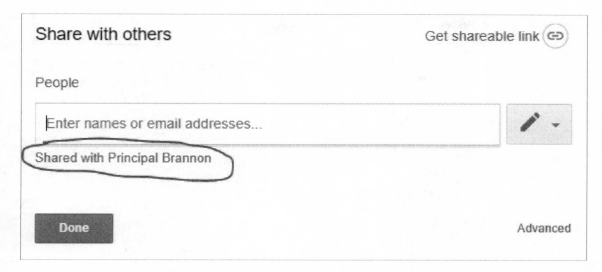

For the second part of this task, we will need to create a chart of all the data. Highlight the entire table.

	A	B	C	D	E	F	G
1	Student	Grade 1	Grade 2	Grade 3	Grade 4	Average	
2	Susan	77	60	55	97	72.25	
3	SMith	55	66	77	88	71.5	
4	Sam	0	76	0	89	41.25	
5	bill	99	98	100	97	98.5	
6	John	88	98	76	94	89	
7	Sam	88	98	67	87	85	
8	Edward	100	99	100	90	97.25	
9	Elisabeth	100	100	99	100	99.66666667	
10							

Now use the Insert Tab, and select Chart…

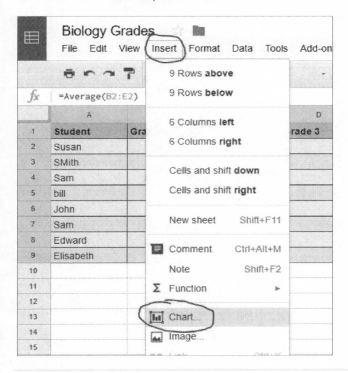

This will open the **Chart Editor** window and paste a chart into the sheet

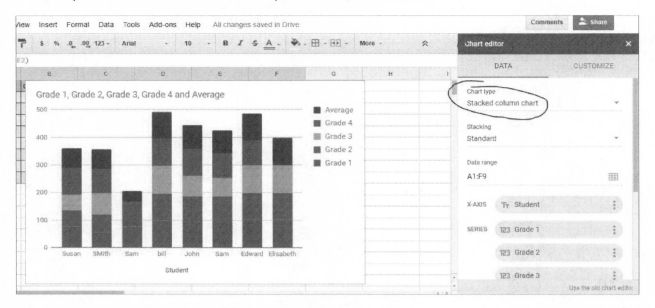

Close the **Chart editor** window and you are done.

Tip: If the question specifically does not tell you to create a certain chart type, then **DO NOT** spend too much time looking for a pretty chart.

Move the Chart out of the way of your data (click and drag it down the screen) and move onto the next task. Your screen should look like this:

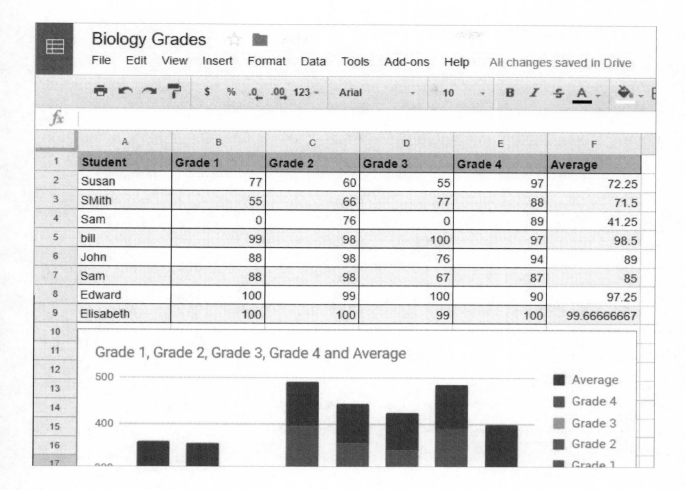

Sample Scenario 2 – Task 3

Task 3 of 3

Principal Brannon was very impressed with your grade sheet, but he would love to see which students are not performing well first.

Sort the **Biology Grades** sheet average score from lowest to highest.
Add a direct comment to Principal Brannon on the cell of the student with the lowest average grade and ask "should we contact their parents?"

With the **Biology Grades** sheet, still open highlight Row 1 (click on the 1)

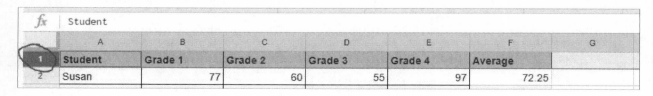

Click the **Filter** button

This will add sorting/filtering options to each of the columns in your sheet:

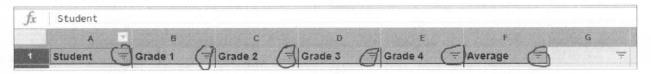

Click on the Filter on the Average cell (F1) and choose **Sort A -> Z**

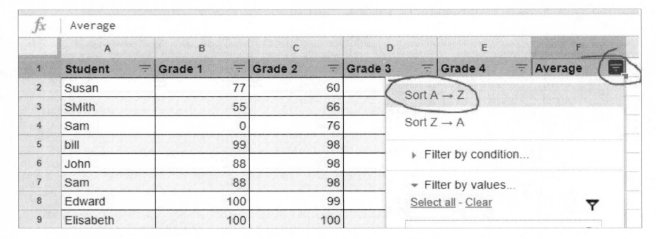

Once Sorted it will place the student with the lowest average score at the top:

	Student	Grade 1	Grade 2	Grade 3	Grade 4	Average
2	Sam	0	76	0	89	41.25
3	SMith	55	66	77	88	71.5
4	Susan	77	60	55	97	72.25
5	Sam	88	98	67	87	85
6	John	88	98	76	94	89
7	Edward	100	99	100	90	97.25
8	bill	99	98	100	97	98.5
9	Elisabeth	100	100	99	100	99.66666667

To add a comment to Sam's abysmal grade, select the cell (F2) and then press the **Comments** button at the top right of the screen. Then click **Comment**

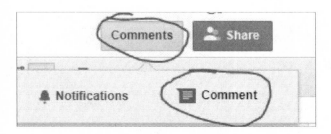

Add the comment to the window and tag Principal Brannon (using their name or email address), press the comment button to save the comment.

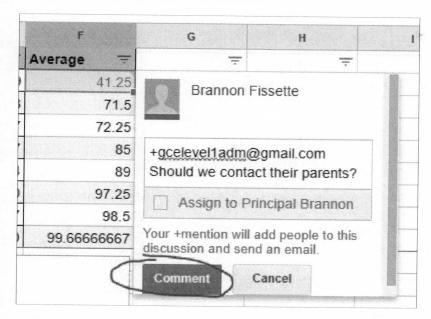

Tip: *To tag someone in a Google Comment use the + key and then add their name or email address.*

Your sheet should look like this now:

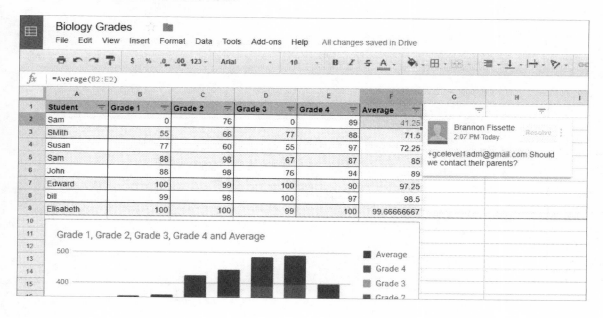

Congratulations, you have finished the Scenario!

Section 4 – Practice Questions

Here are some practice questions that are like the ones found on the Google Certified Educator Level 1 exam. These are NOT on the exam.

Practice Question 1

Multiple Choice Question

Please select 3

Mr. Tarly would love to begin using the Google Suite to create quizzes in his classroom. What are a few of the features in Google Forms that will give Mr. Tarly this ability?

- ☐ Design a logo for his class
- ☐ Automatic grading of Multiple Choice Questions
- ☐ Ability to give feedback on correct or incorrect answers automatically
- ☐ Create a slide deck that the students can work on together
- ☐ Allow students to see missed answers after submitting their exam

Practice Question 2

Drag & Drop Question

Googles Applications can be used for a variety of different purposes. Drag and drop the Application with how it can be used.

How it can be used	Application
1. Create a collaborative document for meeting notes	a. Sheets
2. Organize Data in an easy to view graph	b. YouTube
3. Create video playlists that can be share with students	c. Hangouts
4. Have a video conference with parents that are out of town	d. Sites
5. Have students create a digital portfolio viewable on the internet	e. Docs

Practice Question 3

Multiple Choice Question

Please select 2

Mrs. Stanley's created a YouTube video channel for her History Course. However, one student received an inappropriate comment on one of their videos. What action should Mrs. Stanley take?

- ☐ Look up the offenders IP address and confront them in person
- ☐ Document and report the comment to administration
- ☐ Check the Privacy Setting to ensure the YouTube channel is unlisted or private
- ☐ Respond with an even more nasty comment

Practice Question 4

Multiple Choice Question

Please select 3

Mr. Bentley is going to have his students create a slideshow as a part of their final. What are some of the benefits to using Google slides?

- ☐ Embedding YouTube videos directly into the presentation to make it more exciting
- ☐ Students slide shows can have the same look and feel by using a template
- ☐ Adding audio clips to slides is very easy
- ☐ If needed students can download the presentation into another format (example: PowerPoint)

Practice Question 5

Multiple Choice Question

Please select 5

Mr. Jordan is having issues keeping his students engaged. What are some ways that he can motivate his students using the Google Suite?

- ☐ Schedule a Google Hangout with students in another country
- ☐ Create a YouTube playlist of fun educational videos and share it with the class
- ☐ Create a Choose your own adventure story using Google forms
- ☐ Create a Digital Breakout using a combination of Google Forms and Google Sites
- ☐ Have students do research using the school's library and encyclopedia's.
- ☐ Use Google Slides Audience Q&A to make presentations more interactive

Practice Question 6

Multiple Choice Question

Please select 1

Your school's administration is ready to roll out a digital classroom, but is concerned about digital citizenship. Why should digital citizenship be built into the digital curriculum?

- ☐ Students should have the most followers on Twitter
- ☐ Generate additional revenue through YouTube monetization
- ☐ So, that students are respectful to themselves and others online
- ☐ Students should be able to type 75 words per minute by the end of the semester

Practice Question 7

Drag & Drop Question

Your students are working on a research project for Social Studies using Google Docs. Match the Google Docs feature with this benefit.

Google Docs Feature	**Benefit**
Explore Tool	Students can create diagrams and flow charts of processes from within a Google Document
Suggestions View	Allows students to do research while within the Google Document
Integrated Drawings	A great accessibility option that allows students to dictate text into a Google Document
Comments	Comments can be added to give feedback to students
Voice Typing	Students can proofread and provide suggestions to each other's papers without changing the final copy

Practice Question 8

Multiple Choice Question

Please select 2

Mr. Jones has created a folder within Google Drive and shared it with a group of teachers so that they can easily collaborate on shared documents. What are some of the benefits for using Google Drive?

- ☐ Drive files cannot be recovered easily if deleted
- ☐ Drive files can be viewed on mobile devices using the Google Drive app
- ☐ If a file is renamed within the shared folder everyone will lose access
- ☐ Teachers cannot work on a Google Document at the same time if it is in a shared folder
- ☐ When a new teacher is added to the folder they will automatically have access to everything within that folder with the same rights

Practice Question 9

Multiple Choice Question

Please select 3

Half of Mrs. Steins math class is going on an excursion for two weeks out of state. What Google tools can Mrs. Stein use to continue to communicate with those students?

- ☐ Schedule a video call using Google Hangouts
- ☐ Use Google Classroom to manage assignments for students, so they can access them while away
- ☐ Send letters using Google Snail Mail Service that they can respond to at their own time.
- ☐ Create a Google Group, and use a discussion board to keep in contact

Practice Question 10

Drag & Drop Question

Mrs. Stevens has an idea for a project but is not sure if she wants to use Google Slides or Google Sites to do it. Identify each application benefits to help her decide.

Application	Benefit
Google Slides	Each student can receive the same template as a starting off point
	Students are not limited by content type, and can place long documents on a page
	Projects can be presented to an audience as a standard presentation
	Can be imported into another application such as PowerPoint
	Can be viewed with any web browser or on any smart device with the internet
Google Sites	Content can be organized into different pages for browsing at leisure

Practice Question 11

Multiple Choice Question

Please select 1

Mr. Williamson is attempting to meet with his principal, Mrs. Washington. Mrs. Washington is very busy, what tool can Mr. Williamson use to assist in scheduling the meeting?

- ☐ Call Mrs. Washington using Google hangouts
- ☐ Use Google Classroom to send Mrs. Washington an assignment to meet.
- ☐ Use the 'Fine a Time' feature in google calendar to find a time when Mrs. Washington is available.
- ☐ Knock on Mrs. Washington's door and demand to be seen

Practice Question 12

Multiple Choice Question

Please select 4

Brian has a project due in his Science class. What Google tools can he use to make his project more dynamic?

- ☐ Use Google Drawings to show complex diagrams and relationships between molecules
- ☐ Embed a relevant YouTube video in his Google Doc so the teacher has something exciting to watch.
- ☐ Use sheets to graph data in a visually stunning way
- ☐ Create a Google Site that contains information, links, images and videos that show understanding.
- ☐ Use the explore tool within Google Docs to find images and sources related to the topic

Practice Question 13

Multiple Choice Question

Please select 2

Ms. Pettigrew is trying to teach her students how to organize their work within Google Drive. What Google Drive features should she teach?

- ☐ How to create and name folders for easy navigation
- ☐ How to hide documents in the trash
- ☐ How to add as star to a document or folder for quick access
- ☐ How to delete items in 'Shared With Me' to free up space

Practice Question 14

Drag & Drop Question

Mr. Johnson is teaching a French Language Class and wants to integrate Google tools. Match the Google application feature with its application

Application	Benefit
Google Docs	Embed French YouTube videos
	Translate Documents from English to French
	Embed A Google map of France
Google Hangouts	Schedule a 'Hangout on Air' with students in France
	Invite a guest speaker from France to speak with the class remotely
	Have students create a tourist brochure for a location in France
Google Sites	

Practice Question 15

Multiple Choice Question

Please select 1

Mrs. Whitaker is excited to learn about everything that the Chrome Omnibox can do! Which of the following is NOT a capability of the Chrome Omnibox?

- ☐ Can calculate 2+2
- ☐ Give you the weather in Paris
- ☐ Tell you a joke
- ☐ Convert 50 miles to kilometers

Practice Question 16

Multiple Choice Question

Please select 3

Mr. Pavlo is a math teacher who would like to teach his students how to use Google Sheets to make a balance sheet. What are some features that Mr. Pavlo should share with his students?

- ☐ Using functions such as =Average(…) to calculate data
- ☐ Leveraging the Explore tool to create charts and graphs of data
- ☐ Inserting Audio files to have the spreadsheet read information to the student
- ☐ Adding sheets to organize between different data sets
- ☐ Putting a video clip into the sheet to make it more exciting

Practice Question 17

Multiple Choice Question

Please select 5

Mrs. Mullens would like to start using Google Slides for her presentations but is afraid that slides cannot do everything that she wants to do. To ease her mind, select some of the great features that Google Slides has.

- ☐ Ability to embed videos directly into slides
- ☐ Animation and slide transitions to make the slideshow flow
- ☐ Update the aspect ratio to ensure the slide show fits the screen it is being displayed on.
- ☐ Embed Google Forms and Audio Clips for increase participation
- ☐ Dynamic themes that change the look and feel of the entire slide show
- ☐ Insert Google Drawings of diagrams or flows

Practice Question 18

Multiple Choice Question

Please select 1

Mrs. Blue is trying to share a document with Mr. Yellow, how can Mrs. Blue ensure that Mr. Yellow is notified that he had the document shared with him.

- ☐ Mrs. Blue can call Mr. Yellow and let him know the document is ready
- ☐ Mrs. Blue can send a fax to Mr. Yellow with instructions on how to view the document
- ☐ Mrs. Blue can ensure to check the 'Notify people' checkbox in advanced sharing features
- ☐ Mr. Yellow can yell loudly to Mrs. Blue to ask if the document is available.

Practice Question 19

Multiple Choice Question

Please select 2

Principal Rudolph has decided to create a Google group of all the teachers to help bolster communication. What options does Principal Rudolf have to add teachers to the group?

- ☐ Directly add teachers with their email address
- ☐ Send an email invite to teachers to join the group
- ☐ Tell teachers to join the group with the Google Docs app on their smart phone
- ☐ Post a memo in the break room with instructions on how to join the group
- ☐ Create a signup sheet in google Docs for people who want to join the group

Practice Question 20

Multiple Choice Question

Please select 2

A technology teacher at Silverton High School would like to teach a unit on Digital Citizenship. What takeaways should the students come out of the unit with?

- ☐ How to get more likes on Facebook and retweets on Twitter
- ☐ How to produce the perfect viral video
- ☐ How to act responsibly and safe on the internet
- ☐ How to use proper etiquette online and with technology
- ☐ How to hack in the school's computer to change grades

Section 5 – Practice Questions Answer Key

Practice Question 1 - Answer

Multiple Choice Question

Please select 3

Mr. Tarly would love to begin using the Google Suite to create quizzes in his classroom. What are a few of the features in Google Forms that will give Mr. Tarly this ability?

- ☐ Design a logo for his class   - Google Drawings will allow you to do this but not Google Forms
- ☑ Automatic grading of Multiple Choice Questions
- ☑ Ability to give feedback on correct or incorrect answers automatically
- ☐ Create a slide deck that the students can work on together – Slide decks are the core functionality of Google Slides, not Google Forms
- ☑ Allow students to see missed answers after submitting their exam

Practice Question 2 - Answer

Drag & Drop Question

Googles Applications can be used for a variety of different purposes. Drag and drop the Application with how it can be used.

How it can be used	Application
1. Create a collaborative document for meeting notes	a. Sheets
2. Organize Data in an easy to view graph	b. YouTube
3. Create video playlists that can be share with students	c. Hangouts
4. Have a video conference with parents that are out of town	d. Sites
5. Have students create a digital portfolio viewable on the internet	e. Docs

Practice Question 3 - Answer

Multiple Choice Question

Please select 2

Mrs. Stanley's created a YouTube video channel for her History Course. However, one student received an inappropriate comment on one of their videos. What action should Mrs. Stanley take?

- ☐ Look up the offenders IP address and confront them in person – Dangerous – not a smart choice!
- ☑ Document and report the comment to administration
- ☑ Check the Privacy Setting to ensure the YouTube channel is unlisted or private
- ☐ Respond with an even more nasty comment – Inappropriate and may lead to disciplinary action

Practice Question 4 - Answer

Multiple Choice Question
Please select 3

Mr. Bentley is going to have his students create a slideshow as a part of their final. What are some of the benefits to using Google slides?

- ☑ Embedding YouTube videos directly into the presentation to make it more exciting
- ☑ Students slide shows can have the same look and feel by using a template
- ☐ Adding audio clips to slides is *very* easy – This is a tricky question, even though inserting audio clips is possible in other presentation software it is not possible to do so in Google Slides.
- ☑ If needed students can download the presentation into another format (example: PowerPoint)

Practice Question 5 - Answer

Multiple Choice Question
Please select 5

Mr. Jordan is having issues keeping his students engaged. What are some ways that he can motivate his students using the Google Suite?

- ☑ Schedule a Google Hangout with students in another country
- ☑ Create a YouTube playlist of fun educational videos and share it with the class
- ☑ Create a Choose your own adventure story using Google forms
- ☑ Create a Digital Breakout using a combination of Google Forms and Google Sites
- ☐ Have students do research using the school's library and encyclopedia's – This does not utilize Googles applications and would not be very motivating
- ☑ Use Google Slides Audience Q&A to make presentations more interactive

Practice Question 6 - Answer

Multiple Choice Question
Please select 1

Your school's administration is ready to roll out a digital classroom, but is concerned about digital citizenship. Why should digital citizenship be built into the digital curriculum?

- ☐ Students should have the most followers on Twitter – Has nothing to do with digital citizenship
- ☐ Generate additional revenue through YouTube monetization – Has nothing to do with digital citizenship
- ☑ So, that students are respectful to themselves and others online
- ☐ Students should be able to type 75 words per minute by the end of the semester– Has nothing to do with digital citizenship

Practice Question 7 - Answer

Drag & Drop Question

Your students are working on a research project for Social Studies using Google Docs. Match the Google Docs feature with this benefit.

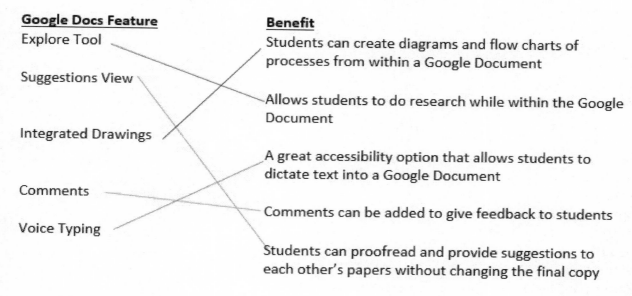

Google Docs Feature

Explore Tool

Suggestions View

Integrated Drawings

Comments

Voice Typing

Benefit

Students can create diagrams and flow charts of processes from within a Google Document

Allows students to do research while within the Google Document

A great accessibility option that allows students to dictate text into a Google Document

Comments can be added to give feedback to students

Students can proofread and provide suggestions to each other's papers without changing the final copy

Practice Question 8 - Answer

Multiple Choice Question

Please select 2

Mr. Jones has created a folder within Google Drive and shared it with a group of teachers so that they can easily collaborate on shared documents. What are some of the benefits for using Google Drive?

- ☐ Drive files cannot be recovered easily if deleted - Drive files can be recovered if accidently deleted
- ☑ Drive files can be viewed on mobile devices using the Google Drive app
- ☐ If a file is renamed within the shared folder everyone will lose access – Even if the file is renamed the shared documents will continued to be shared with the same permissions
- ☐ Teachers cannot work on a Google Document at the same time if it is in a shared folder – Everyone who has edit access to the document can work on it at the same time!
- ☑ When a new teacher is added to the folder they will automatically have access to everything within that folder with the same rights

Practice Question 9 - Answer

Multiple Choice Question

Please select 3

Half of Mrs. Steins math class is going on an excursion for two weeks out of state. What Google tools can Mrs. Stein use to continue to communicate with those students?

- ☑ Schedule a video call using Google Hangouts
- ☑ Use Google Classroom to manage assignments for students, so they can access them while away
- ☐ Send letters using Google Snail Mail Service that they can respond to at their own time. - Using the postal service would be much slower and is not a Google tool
- ☑ Create a Google Group, and use a discussion board to keep in contact

Practice Question 10 - Answer

Drag & Drop Question

Mrs. Stevens has an idea for a project, but is not sure if she wants to use Google Slides or Google Sites to do it. Identify each application benefits to help her decide.

Application	**Benefit**
Google Slides	
Each student can receive the same template as a starting off point	
Projects can be presented to an audience as a standard presentation	
Can be imported into another application such as PowerPoint	
Google Sites	
Students are not limited by content type, and can place long documents on a page	
Can be viewed with any web browser or on any smart device with the internet	
Content can be organized into different pages for browsing at leisure	

Practice Question 11 - Answer

Multiple Choice Question

Please select 1

Mr. Williamson is attempting to meet with his principal, Mrs. Washington. Mrs. Washington is very busy, what tool can Mr. Williamson use to assist in scheduling the meeting?

- ☐ Call Mrs. Washington using Google hangouts – While this is possible, it may not be good to interrupt Mrs. Washington's busy schedule
- ☐ Use Google Classroom to send Mrs. Washington an assignment to meet. – This would assume that Mrs. Washington is in a Google class with Mr. Williamson and is a student, probably not right.
- ☑ Use the 'Fine a Time' feature in google calendar to find a time when Mrs. Washington is available.
- ☐ Knock on Mrs. Washington's door and demand to be seen – Mr. Williamson could do this, but it wouldn't be using a Google tool

Practice Question 12 - Answer

Multiple Choice Question

Please select 4

Brian has a project due in his Science class. What Google tools can he use to make his project more dynamic?

- ☑ Use Google Drawings to show complex diagrams and relationships between molecules
- ☐ Embed a relevant YouTube video in his Google Doc so the teacher has something exciting to watch. – You cannot embed YouTube videos in a Google Doc

☑ Use sheets to graph data in a visually stunning way
☑ Create a Google Site that contains information, links, images and videos that show understanding.
☑ Use the explore tool within Google Docs to find images and sources related to the topic

Practice Question 13 - Answer
Multiple Choice Question
Please select 2
Ms. Pettigrew is trying to teach her students how to organize their work within Google Drive. What Google Drive features should she teach?

☑ How to create and name folders for easy navigation
☐ How to hide documents in the trash – You cannot hide documents in the trash, you can only erase them
☑ How to add as star to a document or folder for quick access
☐ How to delete items in 'Shared with me' to free up space – If you were to delete files in the "Shared with me" folder it could delete them from the owners as well.

Practice Question 14 - Answer
Drag & Drop Question
Mr. Johnson is teaching a French Language Class and wants to integrate Google tools. Match the Google application feature with its application

Application	Benefit
Google Docs	
Translate Documents from English to French	
Have students create a tourist brochure for a location in France	
Google Hangouts	
Schedule a 'Hangout on Air' with students in France	
Invite a guest speaker from France to speak with the class remotely	
Google Sites	
Embed French YouTube videos	
Embed A Google map of France	

Practice Question 15 - Answer
Multiple Choice Question
Please select 1
Mrs. Whitaker is excited to learn about everything that the Chrome Omnibox can do! Which of the following is NOT a capability of the Chrome Omnibox?

☐ Can calculate 2+2 - TRY IT!
☐ Give you the weather in Paris - TRY IT!
☑ Tell you a joke
☐ Convert 50 miles to kilometers- TRY IT!

Practice Question 16 - Answer

Multiple Choice Question

Please select 3

Mr. Pavlo is a math teacher who would like to teach his students how to use Google Sheets to make a balance sheet. What are some features that Mr. Pavlo should share with his students?

- ☑ Using functions such as =Average(...) to calculate data
- ☑ Leveraging the Explore tool to create charts and graphs of data
- ☐ Inserting Audio files to have the spreadsheet read information to the student – You cannot insert audio files into a Google sheet
- ☑ Adding sheets to organize between different data sets
- ☐ Putting a video clip into the sheet to make it more exciting – You cannot insert video clips into a google sheet

Practice Question 17 - Answer

Multiple Choice Question

Please select 5

Mrs. Mullens would like to start using Google Slides for her presentations but is afraid that slides cannot do everything that she wants to do. To ease her mind, select all the great features that Google Slides has.

- ☑ Ability to embed videos directly into slides
- ☑ Animation and slide transitions to make the slideshow flow
- ☑ Update the aspect ratio to ensure the slide show fits the screen it is being displayed on.
- ☐ Embed Google Forms and Audio Clips for increase participation – You cannot embed forms or audio clips into a Google slides presentation
- ☑ Dynamic themes that change the look and feel of the entire slide show
- ☑ Insert Google Drawings of diagrams or flows

Practice Question 18 - Answer

Multiple Choice Question

Please select 1

Mrs. Blue is trying to share a document with Mr. Yellow, how can Mrs. Blue ensure that Mr. Yellow is notified that he had the document shared with him.

- ☐ Mrs. Blue can call Mr. Yellow and let him know the document is ready – This would not be using a Google tool
- ☐ Mrs. Blue can send a fax to Mr. Yellow with instructions on how to view the document– This would not be using a Google tool
- ☑ Mrs. Blue can ensure to check the 'Notify people' checkbox in advanced sharing features
- ☐ Mr. Yellow can yell loudly to Mrs. Blue to ask if the document is available. – This would not be using a Google tool

Practice Question 19 - Answer

Multiple Choice Question

Please select 2

Principal Rudolph has decided to create a Google group of all the teachers to help bolster communication. What options does Principal Rudolf have to add teachers to the group?

- ☑ Directly add teachers with their email address
- ☑ Send an email invite to teachers to join the group
- ☐ Tell teachers to join the group with the Google Docs app on their smart phone — Teachers cannot join a Google group through the Google docs app on their smart phone
- ☐ Post a memo in the break room with instructions on how to join the group — This would not be using a Google tool
- ☐ Create a signup sheet in google Docs for people who want to join the group — While Principal Rudolph could do this, and then enter the data in manually it would defeat the purpose of all the great Google tools!

Practice Question 20 - Answer

Multiple Choice Question

Please select 2

A technology teacher at Silverton High School would like to teach a unit on Digital Citizenship. What takeaways should the students come out of the unit with?

- ☐ How to get more likes on Facebook and retweets on Twitter — While social media etiquette would be good to learn in a digital citizenship course, becoming popular on those platforms would not be a good use of time
- ☐ How to produce the perfect viral video — This could be a fun video editing class, but not a digital citizenship course
- ☑ How to act responsibly and safe on the internet
- ☑ How to use proper etiquette online and with technology
- ☐ How to hack in the school's computer to change grades — Why would anyone want to teach their students this?

Section 6 – Practice Scenarios

The following practice scenarios can be done with any Google account. During the actual exam, you will be asked to use materials located in a folder within Google Drive, the first Scenario will have you create that folder and add a couple of files to it. Good luck!

The answer key section will show you a screen shot of how the scenario should generally look if completed correctly.

Practice Scenario 1 – Task 1

Task 1 of 3

To prepare for the Google Certified Educators Level 1 Exam you need to practice using the Tools. Navigate to https://drive.google.com and do the following.

Within My Drive, create a folder titled **Exam Materials**

Share the Exam Materials Folder with **gcelevel1adm@gmail.com** (Principal Brannon)

Practice Scenario 1 – Task 2

Task 2 of 3

Practice makes perfect, and you need more practice! Within the **Exam Materials** folder create the following Files:

A **Google Doc** titled – *Google Foo and You*

A **Google Slide** titled – Once upon a Google

A **Google Sheet** titled – Google these numbers

Practice Scenario 1 – Task 3

Task 3 of 3

The best way to learn is to do, or something like that. Add the following content to a few of the documents you created.

Within **Google Doc** titled – *Google Foo and You* insert the following text:

> If I can Google, anyone can!

> Seriously, anyone.

Within the **Google Slideshow** titled *Once Upon a Google* create two slides, give each slide the following title (insert a textbox)

> Google Slides 101

All about Google

Open the **Google Sheet** titled – *Google these numbers* and create the following table:

	A	B	C	D
1	Name	Exam 1	Exam 2	Average
2	Bill	98	96	
3	Susan	78	87	
4	Sam	99	82	

Practice Scenario 2 – Task 1

Task 1 of 3

When reviewing a student's work, you realize that their idea is not fully formed and needs some additional information. Inform the student that they need to write more!

Open the **Exam Materials** Folder and open the Google Doc titled *Google Foo and You*
Select the first line of text and add a comment: "Needs more details"
Within the same document select the second line of text and add a direct comment to **Principal Brannon** (**gcelevel1adm@gmail.com**) stating "Please add more information here"

Practice Scenario 2 – Task 2

Task 2 of 3

This document is just so bland. You feel that it could use more exciting imagery!

Open the **Exam Materials** Folder and open the Google Doc titled *Google Foo and You*
Use the **Explore Tool** to insert and image into the document
Use **Google Drawings** to insert Word Art into the document that says, "Google Foo!"

Practice Scenario 2 – Task 3

Task 3 of 3

Wow, this document is really starting to look good. It's too bad the student will not get credit for the assignment. Their name is not on the document, and it does not contain the page number.

Open the **Exam Materials** Folder and open the Google Doc titled *Google Foo and You*
Create a Header for the document. Include your name and the page number. (Note: ensure that the page number is added so that it will update automatically)

Practice Scenario 3 – Task 1

Task 1 of 3

Your student's have just returned from Spring Break, and you want to know what they did with their time off. Create a survey for your students and find out some more information.

Open the **Exam Materials** Folder and create a New Google Form titled "My Spring Break"
Insert three questions:

Question 1:

Where did you go on your spring break? (Short Answer)

Question 2:

What did you enjoy most about Spring Break? (Multiple Choice)
a. The time away from school
b. Being able to sleep in
c. Having some time with the family

Question 3:

Describe a favorite moment that you had on Spring Break. (Paragraph)

Practice Scenario 3 – Task 2

Task 2 of 3

Now that you have a survey created, you would like to get some additional feedback before you send it out.

Open the **Exam Materials** Folder and open the **Google Form** *My Spring Break*
Add **Principal Brannon (gcelevel1adm@gmail.com)** as a collaborator for the Form
Use the form settings to ensure that the form records the students email address and that they can see each other responses.
When completed send the form to **Mrs. Fissette (gcelevel1parent@gmail.com)** so that she can take it.

Practice Scenario 3 – Task 3

Task 3 of 3

You are just about ready to collect results for your survey. You just need to do a little bit more on the back end so that you can see the results clearly.

Open the **Exam Materials** Folder and open the **Google Form** *My Spring Break*
Create a form responses spreadsheet of the survey results
Create a filter and sort the student email addresses in Alphabetical Order as the results come in
Share the responses spreadsheet with Principal Brannon **Principal Brannon (gcelevel1adm@gmail.com)**

Practice Scenario 4 – Task 1

Task 1 of 3

Mrs. Stevens really wants to make her class more exciting, and she heard of this fancy application called YouTube which may help. Help Mrs. Stevens create a fun playlist of videos for her students to enjoy.

Search YouTube for three fun videos and add them to a playlist titled "Fun Videos" – Ensure the playlist is unlisted.
Share the playlist with **Principal Brannon (gcelevel1adm@gmail.com)**

Practice Scenario 4 – Task 2

Task 2 of 3

Mrs. Stevens loves the Discovery Channel, and wants to be made aware of when a new video is added to their YouTube Channel.

Use YouTube to subscribe to the Discovery Channel YouTube Channel

----

Practice Scenario 4 – Task 3

Task 3 of 3

Mrs. Stevens has now realized that her slideshows can be spiced up with her videos! Help her spice up one of her boring presentations.

Within the **Google Slideshow** titled *Once Upon a Google* Insert a YouTube clip from your "Fun Videos" playlist on the first slide
On the second slide create a comment that states "Should we add a video here also?"

Practice Scenario 5 – Task 1

Task 1 of 3

Mrs. White teaches a small class that has had a couple of exams over the short semester. She is tracking her grades in a Google Sheet, but is not sure how to get the students their final grade.

Open the **Exam Materials** Folder and open the **Google Sheet** titled *Google these numbers*
Use the Average Function to average the students Exam 1 and Exam 2 Score
Share the Google Sheet with **Mrs. Fissette (gcelevel1parent@gmail.com)** and **Principal Brannon (gcelevel1adm@gmail.com)**

Practice Scenario 5 – Task 2

Task 2 of 3

Principal Brannon is super impressed with how the students are doing, but would love to see the overall average for each exam and the overall class average as well.

Open the **Exam Materials** Folder and open the **Google Sheet** titled *Google these numbers*
Add the "Class Average" below the last students name (Cell A5)
Average the scores from exam 1, exam 2, and the overall class average using the average function.

Practice Scenario 5 – Task 3

Task 3 of 3

Mrs. Fissette is a bit overwhelmed with all the data and would prefer a more visual representation of the information.

Open the **Exam Materials** Folder and open the **Google Sheet** titled *Google these numbers*
Create a chart of all the information, choose a visually pleasing design.
Copy the chart and paste it into a new **Google Doc** titled "Exam Averages"
Share the **Google Doc** titled *Exam Averages* with **Mrs. Fissette (gcelevel1parent@gmail.com)**.

Practice Scenario 6 – Task 1

Task 1 of 3

Mr. Smithington would like his students to create a digital portfolio using Google sites. To get a feel for it, Mr. Smithington decides to make a template.

Open the **Exam Materials** Folder and create a **New Google Site** titled "My Portfolio" (be sure to use New Google Sites

Set the Theme to 'Impression'

Add a sentence or two to the body of the site

Find a picture using the Insert Image function that represents how you are feeling today

----

Practice Scenario 6 – Task 2

Task 2 of 3

The site is really coming together! Now we need to add some more content.

Open the **Exam Materials** folder and open the **Google Site** titled "My Portfolio".

Create a page titled 'Vacation" under the Home page

> Insert a Map of the United States (hint, use the Map button under the Insert Tab)

Create another page titled "My Videos" under the Home Page

> Find a YouTube video that you like and embed it onto the page

----

Practice Scenario 6 – Task 3

Task 3 of 3

Mr. Smithington is not so sure that his site is up to par and would love some help putting it together.

Open the **Exam Materials** folder and open the **Google Site** titled "My Portfolio".

Add **Mrs. Fissette (gcelevel1parent@gmail.com)** as an editor, and make sure that she is notified.

Practice Scenario 7 – Task 1

Task 1 of 2

Mrs. Reynolds is very excited to try Google Classroom this year, ash she has heard nothing but good things.

Open **Google Classroom** and create a class titled "Google Foo 101" (hint: Ensure that when you sign in that you select Teacher)

Create an announcement on the page with the text "Welcome to Google Foo 101! This is going to be a fun year!"

Add **Mrs. Fissette (gcelevel1parent@gmail.com)** as a Student

---

Practice Scenario 7 – Task 2

Task 2 of 2

Mrs. Reynolds now needs to get her students to work!

Open **Google Classroom** and open the class titled "Google Foo 101"

Create an assignment titled "Google Foo" and attach the Google Doc titled "Google Foo and You". Ensure that each student gets their own copy.

Practice Scenario 8 – Task 1

Task 1 of 2

Principal Fissette loves Google Calendar and the ease that he can create and edit events on it.

Open the **Google Calendar** and create a new Calendar titled "Google Appointments"

Add a 30-minute event titled "Meeting with Mrs. Fissette" onto the Google Appointments calendar at some point in the future

Invite **Mrs. Fissette (gcelevel1parent@gmail.com)** to the meeting

----

Practice Scenario 8 – Task 2

Task 2 of 2

Principal Fissette is also a huge baseball fan and wants to keep track of his favorite team.

Open the **Google Calendar** and use the Browse 'Calendars of Interest' feature to add an MLB team (or other sports team) of your choice to the calendar

----

Practice Scenario 9 – Task 1

Task 1 of 4

Feeling rather ambitious with all this new Google knowledge you have learned, you have decided to create a quiz for your students that grades itself.

Open the **Exam Materials** Folder and create a New **Google Form** titled "Google Foo Quiz"
Insert three questions:

Question 1:
What Google Tool allows you to create websites? (Multiple Choice)
a. Google Sheets
b. Google Docs
c. Google Sites

Question 2:
Google _____ allows you to create quizzes and surveys. (Short Answer)

Question 3:
What Google Certifications can you earn? (Checkbox)
a. Google Certified Educator level 1
b. Google Certified Educator level 2
c. Google Certified Bookkeeper
d. Google Certified Innovator
e. Google Certified Trainer

Practice Scenario 9 – Task 2

Task 2 of 4

Now that you have the questions setup, make the form a quiz!

Open the **Exam Materials** Folder open the **Google Form** titled "Google Foo Quiz"

Make the Google Form a Quiz, that shows the students grade after completing it
Ensure you collect the students email addresses and that they can only take the quiz one time.
Change the Confirmation message to "Thank you for taking my quiz!"

Practice Scenario 9 – Task 3

Task 3 of 4

What good does a quiz do if it doesn't grade itself? Use your new-found knowledge to setup auto-grading of the quiz.

Open the **Exam Materials** Folder and open the **Google Form** titled "Google Foo Quiz"

Using the **Answer key** function for each question set the correct answer and the point value.

Once competed send the quiz to **Mrs. Fissette (gcelevel1parent@gmail.com)** so that she can take it.

Question 1: 10 Points
What Google Tool allows you to create websites? (Multiple Choice)
a. Google Sheets
b. Google Docs
c. Google Sites (CORRECT ANSWER)

Question 2: 20 Points
Google _____ allows you to create quizzes and surveys. (Short Answer)
Forms (CORRECT ANSWER and all other answers incorrect)

Question 3: 30 Points
What Google Certifications can you earn? (Checkbox)
a. Google Certified Educator level 1 (CORRECT ANSWER)
b. Google Certified Educator level 2 (CORRECT ANSWER)
c. Google Certified Bookkeeper
d. Google Certified Innovator (CORRECT ANSWER)
e. Google Certified Trainer (CORRECT ANSWER)

Practice Scenario 9 – Task 4

Task 4 of 4

Now that you have the questions setup, make the form a quiz!

Open the **Exam Materials** Folder open the **Google Form** titled "Google Foo Quiz"

Create a new **Google Sheet** out of the Quiz Results titled "Google Foo Results"
Create a filter that sorts the total grade from Lowest to Highest (A to Z)
Share the Google Sheet results page with **Mrs. Fissette (gcelevel1parent@gmail.com)** with **Can View** rights only.

Practice Scenario 10 – Task 1

Task 1 of 3

Principal Fissette would like to start a Google Group to ease communication with his teachers.

Open **Google Groups** and create a new Group titled "Google Foo Group"

Invite **Mrs. Fissette (gcelevel1parent@gmail.com)** to join the group

Hint: take note of the email address for the group, you will need this later

- -

Practice Scenario 10 – Task 2

Task 2 of 3

Now that Principal Fissette has his Google group created, he wants to send out a welcome email to it.

Open **Google Gmail** and send an email to the Google Foo Group email address

Subject: Welcome to the Google Foo Group!
Body: Welcome! Thank you for joining my group!

- -

Practice Scenario 10 – Task 3

Task 3 of 3

HINT (This task is an example of a level 2 scenario!)

Principal Fissette, loves his new group! He has head of this fun application called Google+ though and would like to explore that as well with his teachers.

Open **Google+** and create a community titled "Google Foo!"
Ensure that the community is Private, and not visible to search
Invite **Mrs. Fissette (gcelevel1parent@gmail.com)** as its first member

- -

Section 7 – Practice Scenarios Answer Key

The answer key will show you a screenshot of how your answer could look. Due to different operating systems and ways of doing things, your screen may look slightly different. However, you should have generally the same result.

Practice Scenario 1 – Task 1 -Answer
Task 1 of 3

To prepare for the Google Certified Educators Level 1 Exam you need to practice using the Tools. Navigate to https://drive.google.com and do the following.

Within My Drive, create a folder titled **Exam Materials**
Share the Exam Materials Folder with **gcelevel1adm@gmail.com** (Principal Brannon)

Folder Created and Shared:

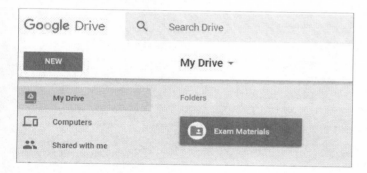

Shared Settings:

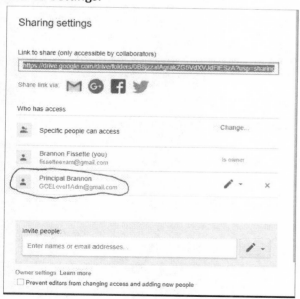

Practice Scenario 1 – Task 2 - Answer

Task 2 of 3

Practice makes perfect, and you need more practice! Within the **Exam Materials** folder create the following Files:

A **Google Doc** titled – *Google Foo and You*
A **Google Slide** titled – Once upon a Google
A **Google Sheet** titled – Google these numbers

Documents Created:

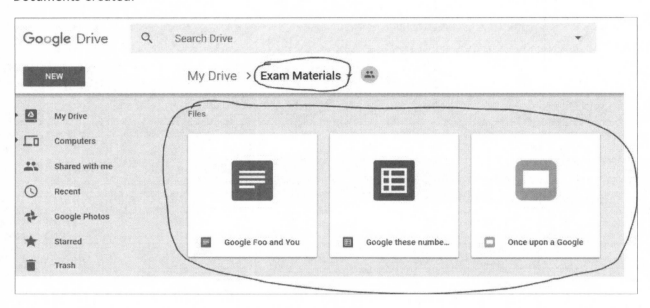

Task 3 of 3

The best way to learn is to do, or something like that. Add the following content to a few of the documents you created.

Within **Google Doc** titled – *Google Foo and You* insert the following text:

> If I can Google, anyone can!

> Seriously, anyone.

Within the Google Slideshow titled *Once Upon a Google* create two slides, give each slide the following title (insert a textbox)

> Google Slides 101

> All about Google

Open the **Google Sheet** titled – *Google these numbers* and create the following table:

	A	B	C	D
1	Name	Exam 1	Exam 2	Average
2	Bill	98	96	
3	Susan	78	87	
4	Sam	99	82	

- -

Google Foo and You

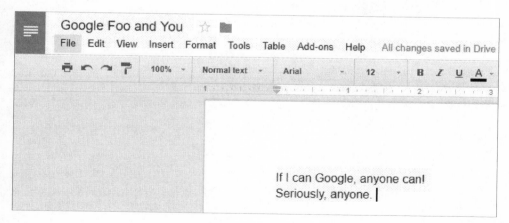

Once Upon a Google

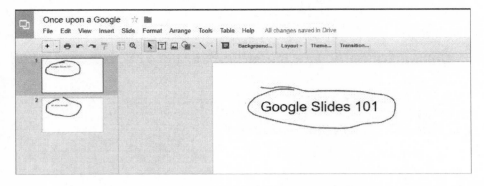

Note: Notice how there is no fancy formatting? The test does not care about aesthetics, do what is asked and move on. There is a time limit!

Google these numbers

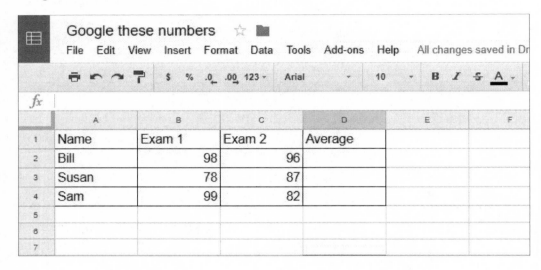

Practice Scenario 2 – Task 1 - Answer

Task 1 of 3

When reviewing a student's work, you realize that their idea is not fully formed and needs some additional information. Inform the student that they need to write more!

Open the **Exam Materials** Folder and open the Google Doc titled *Google Foo and You*

Select the first line of text and add a comment: "Needs more details"

Within the same document select the second line of text and add a direct comment to **Principal Brannon (gcelevel1adm@gmail.com)** stating "Please add more information here"

‒ ‒

Comments:

Note: the second comment is a Direct comment – tagging Principal Brannon **gcelevel1adm@gmail.com** using the

+ key

Practice Scenario 2 – Task 2 - Answer

Task 2 of 3

This document is just so bland. You feel that it could use more exciting imagery!

Open the **Exam Materials** Folder and open the Google Doc titled *Google Foo and You*
Use the **Explore Tool** to insert and image into the document
Use **Google Drawings** to insert Word Art into the document that says "Google Foo!"

Added Imagery:

Tip: The specific picture does not matter, just insert any picture and move on (Timed test!). Also, the color and design of the word art does not matter, just add it and move on!

*Google Tip: To open **Google Drawings** from within a Document use the Insert Menu and then select Drawing...*

Practice Scenario 2 – Task 3 - Answer

Wow, this document is really starting to look good. It's too bad the student will not get credit for the assignment. Their name is not on the document, and it does not contain the page number.

Open the **Exam Materials** Folder and open the Google Doc titled *Google Foo and You*
Create a Header for the document. Include your name and the page number. (Note: ensure that the page number is added so that it will update automatically)

- -

Header Created:

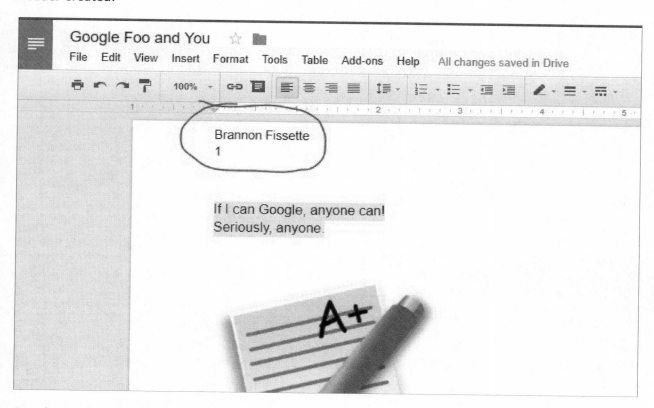

Google Tip: To insert the page number so that it updates automatically use the Insert Menu and select Page number.
Note: Do not worry about placement and making the header look good – Insert the information and move on (Timed Test!)

Practice Scenario 3 – Task 1 - Answer

Task 1 of 3

Your student's have just returned from Spring Break, and you want to know what they did with their time off. Create a survey for your students and find out some more information.

Open the **Exam Materials** Folder and create a New Google Form titled "My Spring Break"

Insert three questions:

Question 1:

Where did you go on your spring break? (Short Answer)

Question 2:

What did you enjoy most about Spring Break? (Multiple Choice)

a. The time away from school

b. Being able to sleep in

c. Having some time with the family

Question 3:

Describe a favorite moment that you had on Spring Break. (Paragraph)

- -

When completed your form should look like this:

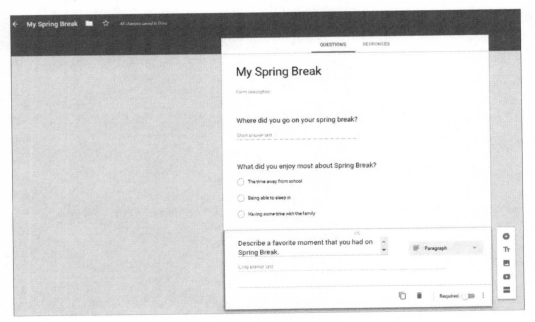

Practice Scenario 3 – Task 2 - Answer

Now that you have a survey created, you would like to get some additional feedback before you send it out.

Open the **Exam Materials** Folder and open the **Google Form** *My Spring Break*
Add **Principal Brannon (gcelevel1adm@gmail.com)** as a collaborator for the Form
Use the form settings to ensure that the form records the students email address and that they can see each other responses.
When completed send the form to **Mrs. Fissette (gcelevel1parent@gmail.com)** so that she can take it.

- -

Share Settings (adding Principal Brannon as a collaborator)

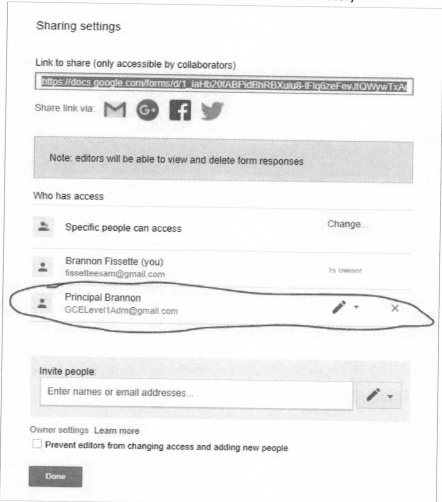

Note: Principal Brannon may already be added if you created the Google Form inside the Exam Materials folder and completed Scenario 1

Correct Form Settings Screen:

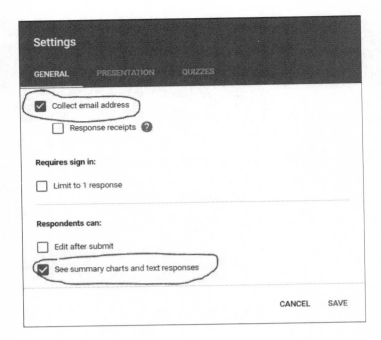

Send Screen:

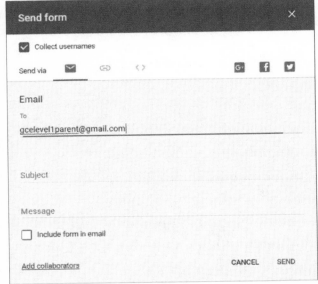

Note: Once you click send, you are done with this task!

Practice Scenario 3 – Task 3 - Answer

Task 2 of 3

You are just about ready to collect results for your survey. You just need to do a little bit more on the back end so that you can see the results clearly.

Open the **Exam Materials** Folder and open the **Google Form** *My Spring Break*
Create a form responses spreadsheet of the survey results
Create a filter and sort the student email addresses in Alphabetical Order as the results come in
Share the responses spreadsheet with Principal Brannon **Principal Brannon (gcelevel1adm@gmail.com)**

- -

Create the form response Spreadsheet by clicking this button in the form Responses Tab:

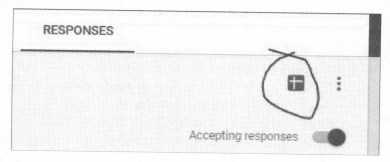

Your Spreadsheet should look like this once filtered and sorted:

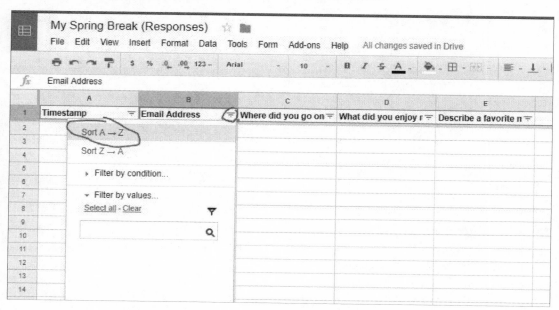

Share Settings Screen:

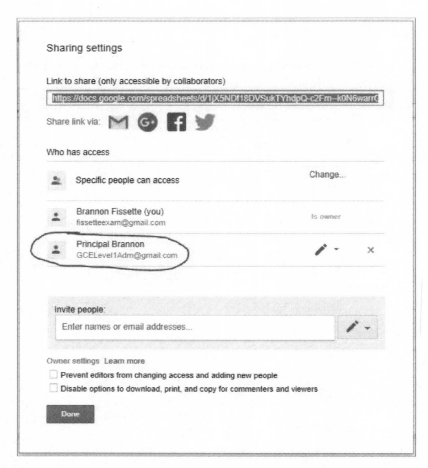

Note: Principal Brannon may already be added if you created the Google Form inside the Exam Materials folder and completed Scenario 1

Practice Scenario 4 – Task 1 - Answer

Task 1 of 3

Mrs. Stevens really wants to make her class more exciting, and she heard of this fancy application called YouTube which may help. Help Mrs. Stevens create a fun playlist of videos for her students to enjoy.

Search YouTube for three fun videos and add them to a playlist titled "Fun Videos" – Ensure the playlist is unlisted.

Share the playlist with **Principal Brannon (gcelevel1adm@gmail.com)**

When you add the first video to a playlist you will be prompted to create a YouTube channel, do this. And then add the video again.

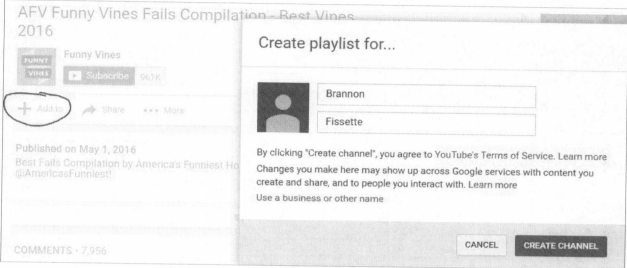

Adding the video:

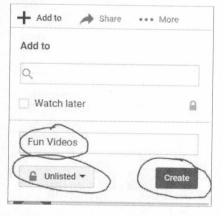

Find two additional videos and add them to the same playlist. Once completed your playlist should look like this (with probably different videos)

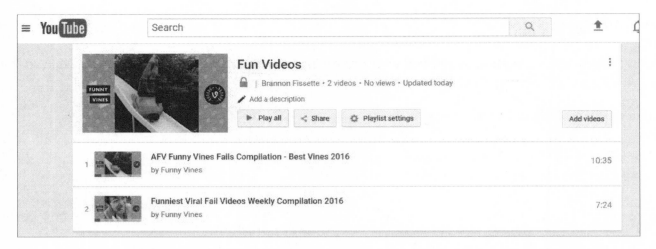

When you Share the playlist with Principal Brannon the share screen should look like this:

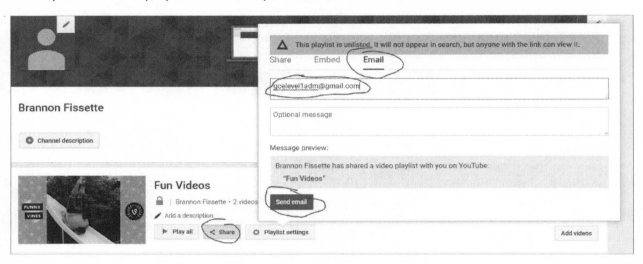

Practice Scenario 4 – Task 2 - Answer

Task 2 of 3

Mrs. Stevens loves the Discovery Channel and wants to be made aware of when a new video is added to their YouTube Channel.

Use YouTube to subscribe to the Discovery Channel YouTube Channel

----

Search and locate the Discovery channel, then it is just as easy as clicking the subscribe button.

Note: Ensure it has the Channel label applied to it before subscribing

Subscribed:

 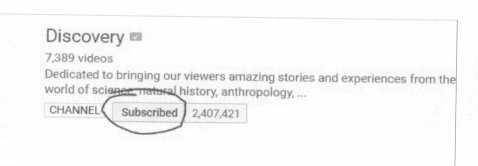

Practice Scenario 4 – Task 3 - Answer

Task 3 of 3

Mrs. Stevens has now realized that her slideshows can be spiced up with her videos! Help her spice up one of her boring presentations.

Within the **Google Slideshow** titled *Once Upon a Google* Insert a **YouTube** clip from your "Fun Videos" playlist on the first slide

On the second slide create a comment that states "Should we add a video here also?"

Slide One Should look like this (With a possibly different video):

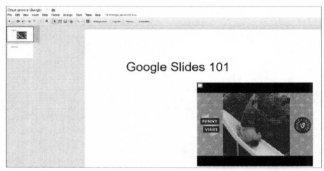

Note: Video placement or content does not matter for the Certification exam – insert the video and move on (Timed Test!)

Slide Two will look like this:

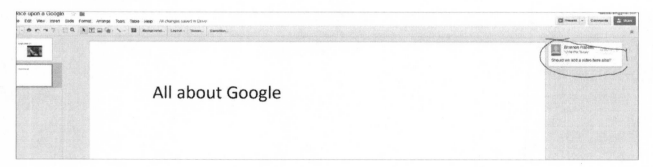

Practice Scenario 5 – Task 1 - Answer

Task 1 of 3

Mrs. White teaches a small class that has had a couple of exams over the short semester. She is tracking her grades in a Google Sheet, but is not sure how to get the students their final grade.

Open the **Exam Materials** Folder and open the **Google Sheet** titled *Google these numbers*

Use the Average Function to average the students Exam 1 and Exam 2 Score

Share the Google Sheet with **Mrs. Fissette (gcelevel1parent@gmail.com)** and **Principal Brannon (gcelevel1adm@gmail.com)**

- -

Google Sheet should look like this:

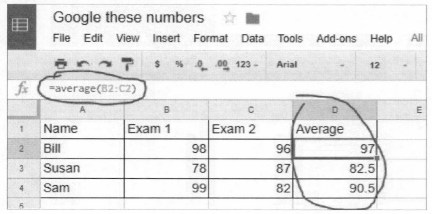

Share Screen:

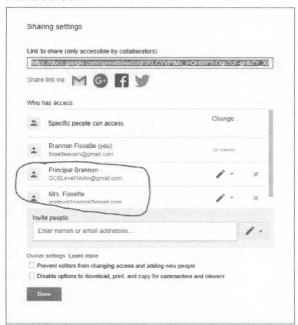

Practice Scenario 5 – Task 2 - Answer

Task 2 of 3

Principal Brannon is super impressed with how the students are doing, but would love to see the overall average for each exam and the overall class average as well.

Open the **Exam Materials** Folder and open the **Google Sheet** titled *Google these numbers*
Add the "Class Average" below the last students name (Cell A5)
Average the scores from exam 1, exam 2, and the overall class average using the average function.

Google Sheet should look like this:

Practice Scenario 5 – Task 3 - Answer

Task 3 of 3

Mrs. Fissette is a bit overwhelmed with all the data and would prefer a more visual representation of the information.

Open the **Exam Materials** Folder and open the **Google Sheet** titled *Google these numbers*
Create a chart of all the information, choose a visually pleasing design.
Copy the chart and paste it into a new **Google Doc** titled "Exam Averages"
Share the **Google Doc** titled *Exam Averages* with **Mrs. Fissette (gcelevel1parent@gmail.com)**.

Highlight all the cells and add a chart – it does not matter what type of chart. Your Google Sheet will look like this (possibly a different chart type):

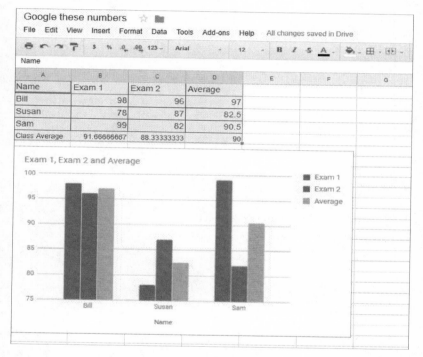

The new Google Document will look like this:

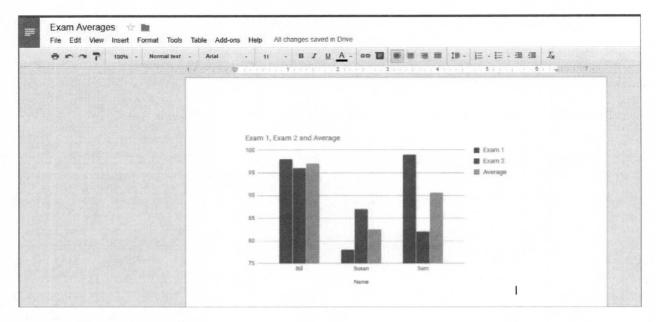

Share Screen will look like this:

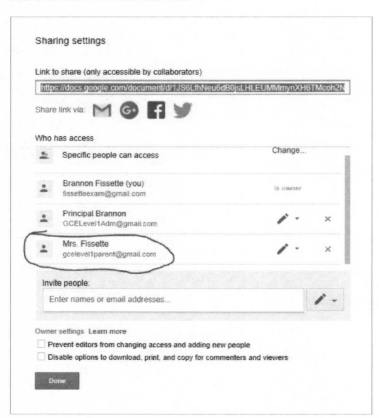

Note: if the Google Doc was created in the Exam Materials folder, Principal Brannon will be listed as an editor also (this is OK!)

Practice Scenario 6 – Task 1 - Answer

Mr. Smithington would like his students to create a digital portfolio using Google sites. To get a feel for it, Mr. Smithington decides to make a template.

Open the **Exam Materials** Folder and create a **New Google Site** titled "My Portfolio" (be sure to use New Google Sites

Set the Theme to 'Impression'

Add a sentence or two to the body of the site

Find a picture using the Insert Image function that represents how you are feeling today

----

The site should look like this once you have completed the task

Practice Scenario 6 – Task 2 - Answer

Task 2 of 4

The site is really coming together! Now we need to add some more content.

Open the **Exam Materials** folder and open the **Google Site** titled "My Portfolio".

Create a page titled 'Vacation" under the Home page

> Insert a Map of the United States (hint, use the Map button under the Insert Tab)

Create another page titled "My Videos" under the Home Page

> Find a YouTube video that you like and embed it onto the page

- -

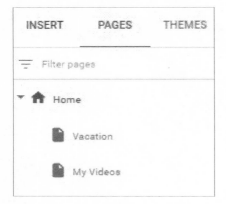

The pages tab should look like the above image.

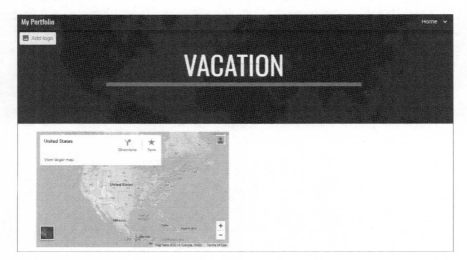

The Vacation page will look like this

The My Videos page will look like this

Task 3 of 3

Mr. Smithington is not so sure that his site is up to par and would love some help putting it together.

Open the **Exam Materials** folder and open the **Google Site** titled "My Portfolio".

Add **Mrs. Fissette (gcelevel1parent@gmail.com)** as an editor, and make sure that she is notified.

The Share button on Google sites is next to the Publish button

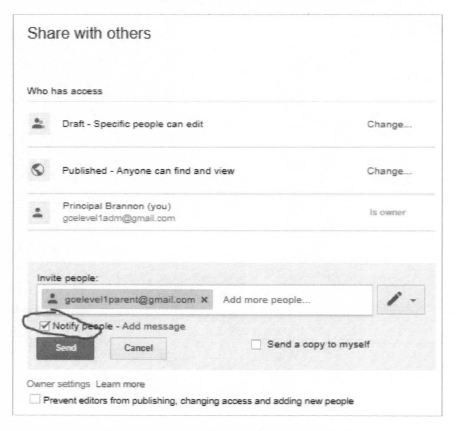

Ensure that the "Notify people" checkbox is checked

Mrs. Reynolds is very excited to try Google Classroom this year, ash she has heard nothing but good things.

Open **Google Classroom** and create a class titled "Google Foo 101" (hint: Ensure that when you sign in that you select Teacher)

Create an announcement on the page with the text "Welcome to Google Foo 101! This is going to be a fun year!"

Add **Mrs. Fissette (gcelevel1parent@gmail.com)** as a Student

----

The Class Stream should look like the above image (possibly with a different Theme)

The Students tab should look like the above image

Practice Scenario 7 – Task 2 - Answer
Task 2 of 2

Mrs. Reynolds is very excited to try Google Classroom this year, ash she has heard nothing but good things.

Open **Google Classroom** and open the class titled "Google Foo 101"

Create an assignment titled "Google Foo" and attach the Google Doc titled "Google Foo and You". Ensure that each student gets their own copy.

- -

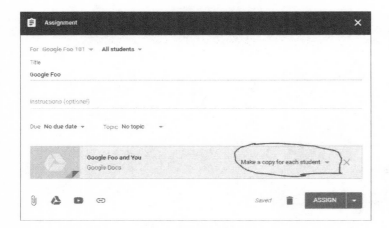

The created assignment should look like the above image. Ensure to select the "Make a copy for each student" option from the dropdown.

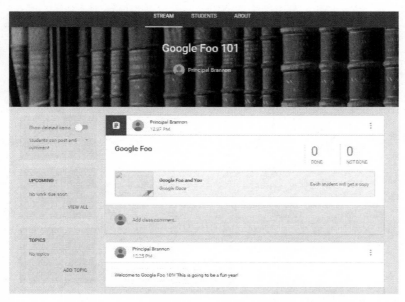

Once you click the "Assign" button your classroom should now look like the above image.

Task 1 of 2

Principal Fissette loves Google Calendar and the ease that he can create and edit events on it.

Open the **Google Calendar** and create a new Calendar titled "Google Appointments"

Add a 30-minute event titled "Meeting with Mrs. Fissette" onto the Google Appointments calendar at some point in the future

Invite **Mrs. Fissette (gcelevel1parent@gmail.com)** to the meeting

----

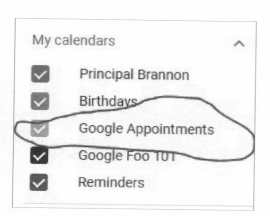

You will see the created calendars listed on the left side of the screen if done properly

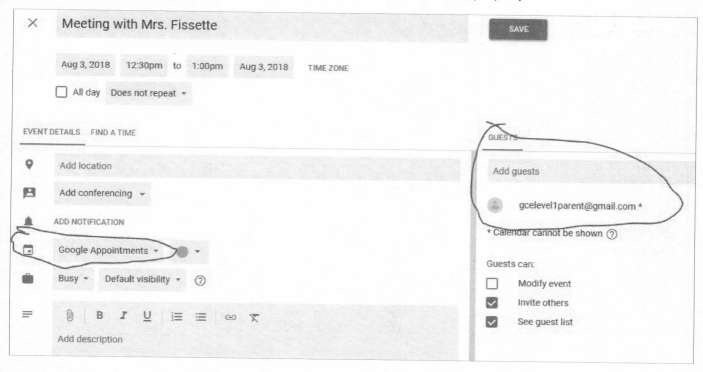

When you create the event ensure that it is on the "Google Appointments" calendar and that you add Mrs. Fissette as a Guest

Practice Scenario 8 – Task 2 - Answer

Task 2 of 2

Principal Fissette is also a huge baseball fan and wants to keep track of his favorite team.

Open the **Google Calendar** and use the Browse 'Calendars of Interest' feature to add an MLB team (or other sports team) of your choice to the calendar

----

The 'Browse calendars of interest' feature can be found next to "Add a Friends Calendar"

This is how the 'Browse calendars of interest' page looks when navigating Baseball teams

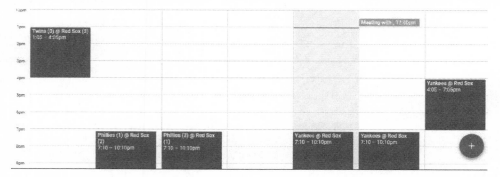

When completed you should have games listed on your calendar (may have to go into the future to see future games)

Task 1 of 4

Feeling rather ambitious with all this new Google knowledge you have learned, you have decided to create a quiz for your students that grades itself.

Open the **Exam Materials** Folder and create a New **Google Form** titled "Google Foo Quiz"
Insert three questions:

Question 1:
What Google Tool allows you to create websites? (Multiple Choice)
a. Google Sheets
b. Google Docs
c. Google Sites

Question 2:
Google _____ allows you to create quizzes and surveys. (Short Answer)

Question 3:
What Google Certifications can you earn? (Checkbox)
a. Google Certified Educator level 1
b. Google Certified Educator level 2
c. Google Certified Bookkeeper
d. Google Certified Innovator
e. Google Certified Trainer

What Google Tool allows you to create websites?

○ Google Sheets

○ Google Docs

○ Google Sites

Google _____ allows you to create quizzes and surveys.

Short answer text

Each question should be formatted like the above image.

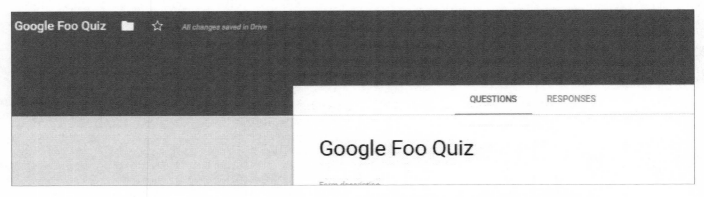

The top of the form should look like the above image. Ensure that the Title is "Google Foo Quiz" and the document is not saved as "Untitled Form"

Task 2 of 4

Now that you have the questions setup, make the form a quiz!

Open the **Exam Materials** Folder open the **Google Form** titled "Google Foo Quiz"

Make the Google Form a Quiz, that shows the students grade after completing it
Ensure you collect the students email addresses and that they can only take the quiz one time.
Change the Confirmation message to "Thank you for taking my quiz!"

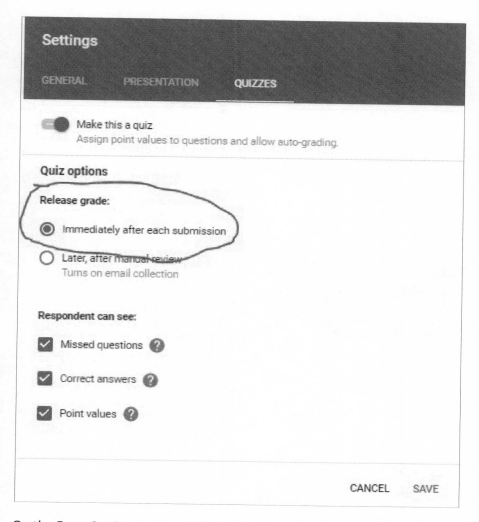

On the Form Settings ensure that "Make this a quiz" is checked as well as releasing the grade immediately after each submission

(HINT: If the question does not ask you to change any other settings, don't – leave them as the default.)]

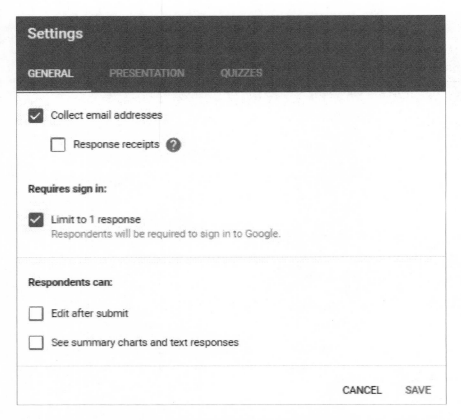

The Google form General settings should look like the above image. Ensure the checkbox next to "Collect email addresses" and "Limit to 1 response" are checked

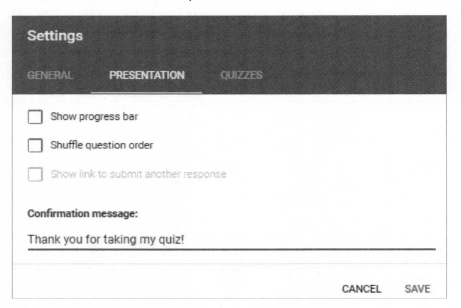

The Confirmation message can be found under the Presentation settings under the Google Form settings. Ensure that it looks like the above image.

Practice Scenario 9 – Task 3 – Answer Key

Task 3 of 4

What good does a quiz do if it doesn't grade itself? Use your new-found knowledge to setup auto-grading of the quiz.

Open the **Exam Materials** Folder and open the **Google Form** titled "Google Foo Quiz"

Using the **Answer key** function for each question set the correct answer and the point value.

Once competed send the quiz to **Mrs. Fissette (gcelevel1parent@gmail.com)** so that she can take it.

Question 1: 10 Points
What Google Tool allows you to create websites? (Multiple Choice)
a. Google Sheets
b. Google Docs
c. Google Sites (CORRECT ANSWER)

Question 2: 20 Points
Google _____ allows you to create quizzes and surveys. (Short Answer)
Forms (CORRECT ANSWER and all other answers incorrect)

Question 3: 30 Points
What Google Certifications can you earn? (Checkbox)
a. Google Certified Educator level 1 (CORRECT ANSWER)
b. Google Certified Educator level 2 (CORRECT ANSWER)
c. Google Certified Bookkeeper
d. Google Certified Innovator (CORRECT ANSWER)
e. Google Certified Trainer (CORRECT ANSWER)

- -

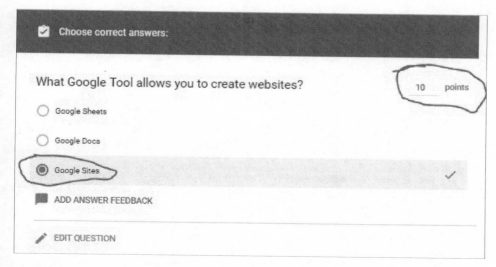

Question 1 Answer Key should look like the above image

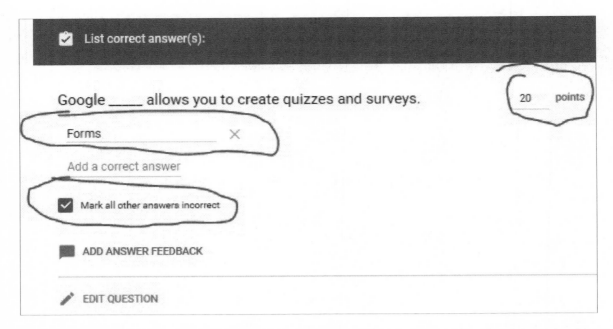

The fill in the blank answer key should look like the above image. Ensure that the point value is correct and the "Mark all other answers as incorrect" box is checked.

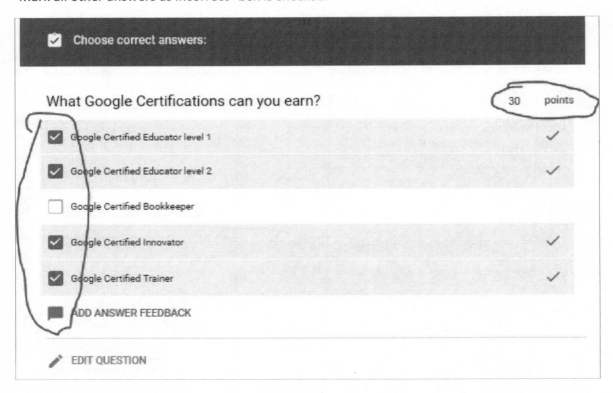

The select more than one option question should have each correct answer checked. Ensure that the point value is also correct.

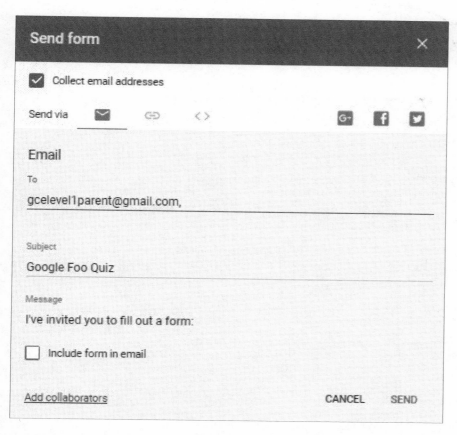

Using Google Forms send function ensure that you have spelled Mrs. Fissette's email address correctly before you send the form.

Task 4 of 4

Now that you have the questions setup, make the form a quiz!

Open the **Exam Materials** Folder open the **Google Form** titled "Google Foo Quiz"

Create a new **Google Sheet** out of the Quiz Results titled "Google Foo Results"
Create a filter that sorts the total grade from Lowest to Highest (A to Z)
Share the Google Sheet results page with **Mrs. Fissette (gcelevel1parent@gmail.com)** with **Can View** rights only.

	QUESTIONS	RESPONSES		Total points:	60

0 responses

Accepting responses ⬤

Scores

Waiting for 1 response

SEND EMAIL REMINDER

gcelevel1parent@gmail.com

Waiting for responses

On the Form responses tab, select the Green create a Spreadsheet button

Select response destination ✕

⦿ Create a new spreadsheet   Google Foo Results   Learn More

◯ Select existing spreadsheet

CANCEL   CREATE

Ensure to rename the new spreadsheet as "Google Foo Results"

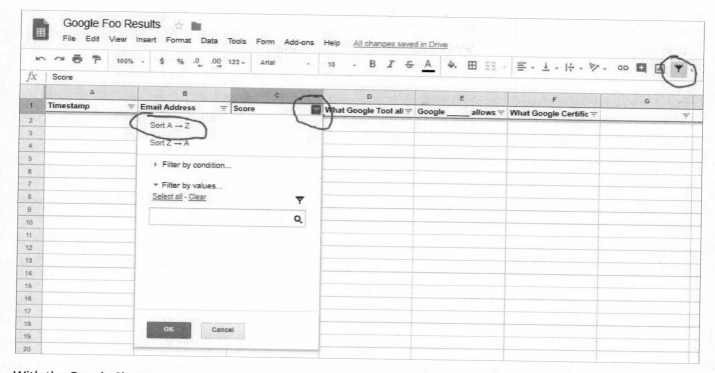

With the Google Sheet opened, turn on the filter and sort the 'Score' column from A -> Z

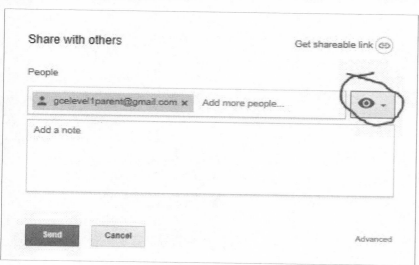

Share the Google Sheet with Mrs. Fissette, ensure that the permissions are set to "Can View"

Practice Scenario 10 – Task 1 – Answer Key

Task 1 of 3

Principal Fissette would like to start a Google Group to ease communication with his teachers.

Open Google Groups and create a new Group titled "Google Foo Group"

Invite Mrs. Fissette (gcelevel1parent@gmail.com) to join the group

Hint: take note of the email address for the group, you will need this later

- -

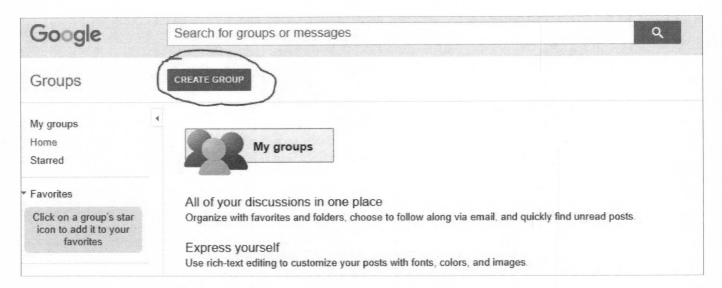

Use the "CREATE GROUP" button found on http://Groups.Google.com

Before you create the group, take note of the email address it has created.

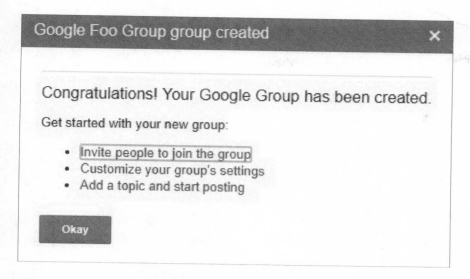

When the Group is created use the "Invite people to join the group" link on the confirmation page.

If you accidently hit "Okay" or close the window you can also go to "Manage" and then "Invite Members" – See the below images.

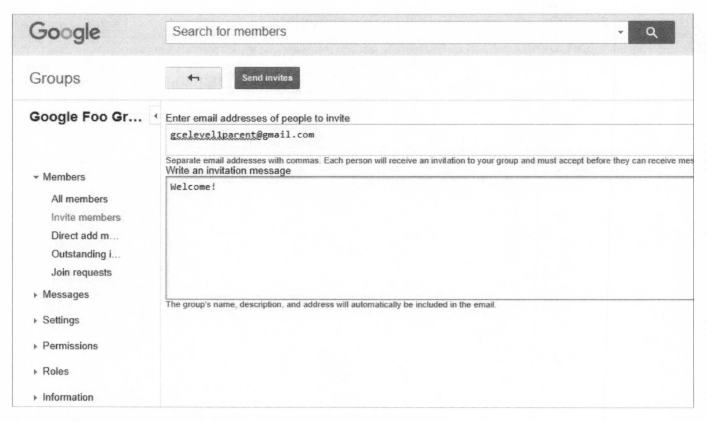

Send Mrs. Fissette the invite, you can place any text into the invitation message.

Task 2 of 3

Now that Principal Fissette has his Google group created, he wants to send out a welcome email to it.

Open Google Gmail and send an email to the Google Foo Group email address

Subject: Welcome to the Google Foo Group!
Body: Welcome! Thank you for joining my group!

- -

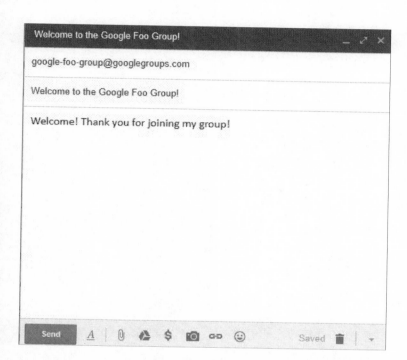

Format the email to the Google group like the above image. If you forgot the group email address, Open **Google Groups**, find the 'Google Foo Group' and select the About link to display it. See the below images for a reference.

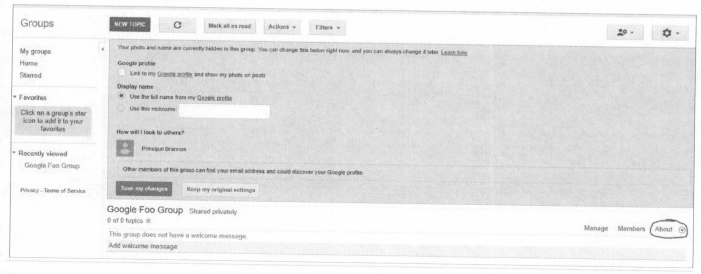

Task 3 of 3

HINT (This task is an example of a level 2 scenario!)

Principal Fissette, loves his new group! He has head of this fun application called Google+ though and would like to explore that as well with his teachers.

Open **Google+** and create a community titled "Google Foo!"

Ensure that the community is Private, and that not visible to search

Invite **Mrs. Fissette (gcelevel1parent@gmail.com)** as its first member

- -

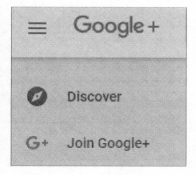

If this is your first time using Google+ you will need to join it, click the Join Google+ button.

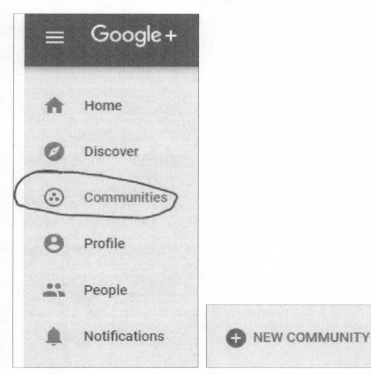

Navigate to **Communities** and select the "Create Community" button

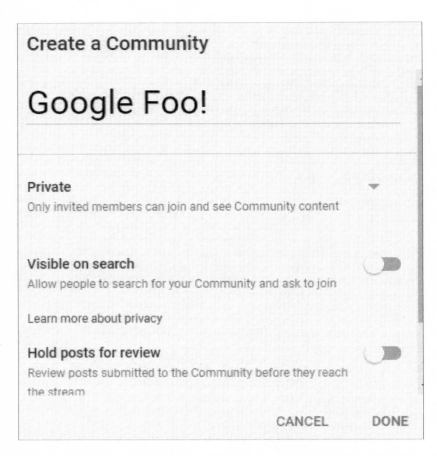

The "Create a Community" window should look like the above image.

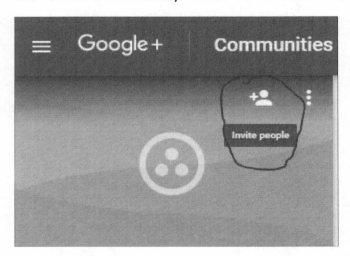

Select the "Invite people" button to invite Mrs. Fissette

Use the Link invite to invite Mrs. Fissette – Copy the link. And open **Gmail**

Email Mrs. Fissette the link to the Google+ community. You can put anything you like in the subject line.

Section 8 – Notes

The Google Certified Educator Level 1 is a timed exam. Do not underestimate how long each scenario will take to complete. Some have just one or two tasks while others can have up to five tasks to complete.

Practice, play with all the Google Suite tools. The exam will cover at minimum these:

Google Drive
Google Docs
Google Slides
Google Sheets
Google Sites
Google Forms
Google Classroom
Google Hangouts
Gmail
Google Calendar
Google Groups
YouTube

If possible, take the test on a computer with two monitors. You will be able to have the Scenario Questions open on one monitor and work on the scenarios in the other. This will save time, from clicking back and forth between windows to refresh your memory on a task.

Do not stress out too much, while you do need an 80% to pass if you fail the first time you can retake the exam after 14 days

Do not get stuck on one question or scenario for too long, use the "Review" button on questions you are having trouble with and go back to it at the end.

When working on the scenarios do not harp on aesthetics. The test uses algorithms to grade and does not care how visually appealing your Google site or Slide show is. Do the minimum and move onto the next task. The three hours goes quick!

Notes

<u>Notes</u>

Notes

<u>Notes</u>

Notes

Notes

Made in the USA
Lexington, KY
09 September 2019